American Red Cross

BABYSITTER'S HANDBOOK

The following organizations provided expert review
of the *Babysitter's Handbook*:

BOYS & GIRLS CLUBS OF AMERICA

BOY SCOUTS OF AMERICA

GIRL SCOUTS®

Y

StayWell

StayWell

Important certification information

American Red Cross certificates may be issued upon successful completion of a training program, which uses this textbook as an integral part of the course. By itself, the text material does not constitute comprehensive Red Cross training. In order to issue ARC certificates, your instructor must be authorized by the American Red Cross, and must follow prescribed policies and procedures. Make certain that you have attended a course authorized by the Red Cross. Ask your instructor about receiving American Red Cross certification, or contact your local chapter for more information.

Copyright ©1998 by The American National Red Cross

This participant's handbook is an integral part of the American Red Cross Babysitter's Training course. By itself, it does not constitute complete and comprehensive training for first aid. Please contact your Red Cross chapter for further information on this course.

The emergency care procedures outlined in this book reflect the standard of knowledge and accepted emergency practices in the United States at the time this book was published. It is the reader's responsibility to stay informed of changes in the emergency care procedures.

Printed in the United States of America

Composition by MKR Design, Inc.
Printing/binding by Mail-Well Graphics

StayWell
263 Summer Street
Boston, MA 02210

Library of Congress Cataloging in Publication Data

ISBN 0-8151-3685-4

02 / 9 8 7

Acknowledgments

The Babysitter's Training course and this handbook were developed and produced through a joint effort of the American Red Cross and Mosby. Many individuals shared in the overall process in supportive, technical, and creative ways. This course could not have been developed without the dedication of both volunteer and paid staff. Their commitment to excellence made this course and handbook possible.

The Babysitter's Training Development team at American Red Cross national headquarters responsible for designing the course and writing this handbook included: Mary Ann Polacek, RN, MSN, MPPM, Project Team Leader; Rhonda Starr, Project Manager; S. Elizabeth White, MAEd, ATC, Senior Associate; Tab Bates, NREMT-B, Jon-Patrick Ewing, Jane Howard, RN, BA, Jane Moore, Paul Stearns, Associates, New Products and Services Development; John Hendrickson, MBA, Business Planning and Development; Lynn Kocik Keefe, Beverly Hoover, Don May, Associates, Products and Services Support; Earl Harbert, Manager, Contract Management. Administrative support was provided by Betty Williams-Butler and Vivian Mills.

In addition, the following American Red Cross national headquarters staff provided guidance and review: Mark Robinson, Vice President, Chapter Operations and Martin Sarsfield, Analyst, Risk Management.

The Mosby Editorial and Production Team included: Claire Merrick, Editor-in-Chief; Doug Bruce, Director Book Operations; Christine Ambrose, Managing Editor; Ross Goldberg, Editorial Project Manager; Shannon Bates and Nadine Steffan, Project Supervisors; Jerry Wood, Director of Manufacturing; Betty Mueller, Manufacturing Manager; Theresa Fuchs, Manager, Media Relations. Mosby also thanks Stacey Wildenberg and Nancy Peterson for their efforts with the development of this project.

Special thanks go to Tom Lochhaas, Developmental Editor; Lynette Long, PhD, Pamela Jean Frable, ND, RN, Katherine Diseroad Watts RN, BSN, CHES, contributing writers; MAD, Inc., focus group and pilot test researcher; MKR Design Inc., cover and interior designers, and Patricia Brangle, Patrick Merrill, Hugo Cruz, Patricia Sweeney, and Karen Schmidt, Illustrators.

Guidance and review were also provided by members of the American Red Cross Babysitter's Training Advisory Committee:

Robert B. Barry
Volunteer Instructor
American Red Cross
Centre Communities Chapter
State College, Pennsylvania

Terri L. Badour, MS, CHES
Director, Product Development
American Red Cross
Metropolitan Atlanta Chapter
Atlanta, Georgia

Kathryn M. Cufari, MS Ed
Education Specialist
American Red Cross
Greater Rochester Chapter
Rochester, New York

Marlo I. Foltz
Director, Health and Safety Services
American Red Cross
Badger Chapter
Madison, Wisconsin

R. J. H. Nina Krantz
Health and Safety Advisor;
Zone 4 Consultant
American Red Cross
Office of the Hub Manager
Fort Belvoir, Virginia

Kathryn M. Hope, MS
Station Manager II
American Red Cross
Armed Forces Emergency
Services Station
Schweinfurt, Germany

Carole T. Riley
Volunteer—Youth Services
American Red Cross
Bay Area Chapter
San Francisco, California

Guidance and review were also provided by the following youth at the American Red Cross:

Hilary Douglas

Natalie Fakhouri

Janette Hardin

Navin Narayan

Helen E. Storey

Coretta Thompson

Christine Vanderbeek

Linda C. Yang

External review was provided by the following organizations and individuals:

Cheryl L. Adams, LPN
Associate Director Health Services
American Red Cross
West Central Michigan Chapter
Grand Rapids, Michigan

Meredith K. Appy
Vice President for Public Education
National Fire Protection Association
Quincy, Massachusetts

Susan P. Brokaw
Program Specialist—Youth Services
American Red Cross
Dallas Area Chapter
Dallas, Texas

Stephanie D. Bryn
Co-Director, Injury and Violence
Prevention Program
Health Resources and Services
Administration
Maternal and Child Health Bureau
Rockville, Maryland

Sandra L. Bugg, MA
Membership and Program Consultant
Girl Scouts of the U.S.A.
New York, New York

Kenneth R. Darden
Director, Prevention Services
Boys and Girls Clubs of America
Atlanta, Georgia

Victoria M. Duran, MSW, LCSW
Chicago, Illinois

Lynn F. Durback, RN, BSN, MBA, CSPI
Supervisor of Operations
West Virginia Poison Center
Charleston, West Virginia

- Fay Flowers, RN, MEd
- Director Health and Community Outreach
- American Red Cross
- Southeastern Michigan Chapter
- Detroit, Michigan
-
- Janie W. Garrett
- Director—Youth Services
- American Red Cross
- Dallas Area Chapter
- Dallas, Texas
-
- William M. Griffin
- Director, Philmont Training Center
- Boy Scouts of America
- Cimarron, New Mexico
-
- Carolyn Jefferson-Jenkins, PhD
- Vice President—Curriculum
- Junior Achievement, Inc.
- Colorado Springs, Colorado
-
- Barbara Larson, RN, MEd
- Director of Education
- CM Healthcare Resources, Inc.
- Deerfield, Illinois
-
- Sharon G. Lewis, MBA
- Volunteer
- American Red Cross
- Greater Hartford Chapter
- Farmington, Connecticut
-
- Diana Meltzer, MEd
- Coordinator, Educational
- Outreach Services
- The Lab School of Washington
- Washington, DC
-
- Lawrence D. Newell, EdD, NREMT-P
- Newell Associates, Inc.
- Ashburn, Virginia
- Adjunct Professor; Emergency Medical
- Technologies
- Northern Virginia Community College
- Annandale, Virginia

v

Robert W. Schafermeyer, MD
Board Member
American College of Emergency
Physicians
Dallas, Texas
Associate Chairman of Emergency
Medicine
Carolinas Medical Center
Charlotte, North Carolina

Lana M. Shaughnessy, MA
Education Program Specialist
Bureau of Indian Affairs/Office of
Indian Education Programs
Washington, DC

Sally L. Smith, MA
Founder/Director
The Lab School of Washington
Washington, DC

Cindy Tait, RN, MPH, PHN
President
Center for Healthcare Education, Inc.
Riverside, California

- Barbara A. Taylor
- Associate Director
- YMCA of the USA
- Chicago, Illinois

- Elaine A. Tyrrell, MS
- Program and Management Analyst
- U.S. Consumer Product Safety
- Commission
- Washington, DC

- Ann Validzic
- Research Assistant
- National SAFE KIDS Campaign
- Washington, DC

- Kathleen E. Vos, PhD
- Professor
- Program Development Specialist
- 4-H Youth Development
- Department of Youth Development
- University of Wisconsin-Extension
- Cooperative Extension
- Madison, Wisconsin

- Lori A. Wildenberg
- Eden Prairie, Minnesota

CONTENTS

First Aid Action Plans, ... 107

Glossary, ... 142

Index, ... 146

iNTRODUCTiON
To BABYSiTTiNG
● ● ●

Be Safe and Responsible

What makes a "good" babysitter who is asked back again and again? There is no one characteristic that makes someone a good babysitter. Instead, a good babysitter successfully combines the knowledge and skills associated with leadership, safety and safe play, basic care, first aid, and professionalism. This course has been designed around these five major themes. Throughout the American Red Cross Babysitter's Handbook, we use five icons, or symbols, to remind you of the major themes of babysitting.

The five icons are—

The star represents leadership. A babysitter shows leadership when he or she ensures the safety of children, encourages appropriate play, provides basic care and first aid, and demonstrates professionalism.

The stop sign reminds you to stop and think about all of your actions when babysitting. Do your part to prevent **accidents** and illnesses by identifying solutions to safety-related problems.

The heart represents basic care. A babysitter's basic care responsibilities include cleanliness and personal **hygiene**, feeding, diapering, **toileting**, rest, sleep, holding, and dressing.

The bandage represents the first aid information you will learn in this course. Using the action steps **Check-Call-Care**, babysitters can decide how to respond to an emergency.

The briefcase reminds you to act like a professional. Babysitters use the symbols of the star, stop sign, heart, bandage, and briefcase to remind them of the qualities necessary to achieve a successful babysitting business.

Babysitting Cast of Characters

By enrolling in the American Red Cross Babysitter's Training course, you are taking an important first step toward becoming a safe, responsible, and successful babysitter. All the characters below represent safe, responsible, and successful babysitters. Their job is to help you gain knowledge and skills to become a really great babysitter. You will see these characters throughout this Babysitter's Handbook, where they will guide you on the road to becoming a skilled and confident babysitter.

Hi! I'm your babysitting mascot! I'll be with you through the whole book!

How to Use the American Red Cross Babysitter's Handbook

This Babysitter's Handbook is to be used when taking the American Red Cross Babysitter's Training course. As you do the class activities, your instructor will direct you to certain pages in this book. Go ahead and write on the Activity Pages. This is YOUR book.

You should keep on using this Babysitter's Handbook after the course whenever you babysit. Look in the back of this book for First Aid Action Plans, starting on p. 107. These plans explain how to take care of different kinds of accidents and illnesses children may experience. The First Aid Action Plans are easy to find because of the orange border on the edges of the pages.

You may see some words that you do not understand. We have highlighted in **red type** those terms that you might need more information about and have explained them in the glossary at the back of this book.

Just for fun, the Babysitter's Handbook also contains some games and puzzles. They will test your babysitting knowledge and skills. Try them out at home after your lessons in class. You'll enjoy them and learn some more too!

Interviewing Tips

Before taking a babysitting job, always interview the family first. The Family Interview Form on pp.5–7 lists questions you should ask. While you are interviewing the family to see if you want to babysit for them, they are also interviewing you. This way, everyone can decide if you and the job are the right match.

Make some copies of the Family Interview Form, and take one with you the first time you work with a family. Be sure to look over the form BEFORE you get there so that you remember what's on it. But don't just hand it to the parents or guardians to fill out. It's better to ask the questions yourself so that you can ask about any problems or special things that might come up.

Feel free to ask a lot of questions to make sure you find out everything you need to know to do a good job. Relax and be friendly. Tell the parents or guardians about yourself: how old you are, where you go to school, why you want the job, and what you like best about taking care of children. Then you can start asking questions about the family.

The interview is your chance to make sure the job is right for you. You'll also find out everything you need to know to be a GREAT babysitter for the family—the kind of babysitter the children love to be with and who is asked back again and again!

Family Interview Form

Family Information and Emergency Numbers

Family name:

Phone number:

Address:

Child's name	Age
1. _____	
2. _____	
3. _____	

Phone number where parent or guardian will be:

Cellular phone number:

Neighbor's name and phone number:

Local emergency phone number:

Doctor's name:

Doctor's phone number:

Poison Control Center (PCC):

Household Rules and Discipline

What are the rules in the household? How would you like me to handle misbehavior?	
Do the children need to complete any chores? If so, what are they?	

Safety and Play

Will you take me on a tour of the house so I can fill out the Safety Inspection Checklist?	
Does your family have a fire escape plan? Do your children know Stop, Drop, and Roll?	
Does the family have any pets? Do I need to care for these pets?	
What are the family's rules for play? What are the children's favorite play activities? What play areas and activities are off-limits or restricted?	

Basic Care

How do you want me to handle handwashing and brushing and flossing teeth?	
What can the children eat and drink? Will I be preparing any simple meals? Do the children have any food allergies?	
What are the routines for diapering and using the toilet? Where are the supplies kept? Where do you want me to put the dirty diapers?	

What are the routines for quiet time, bedtime, and naps? When is bedtime? Do the children have a favorite bedtime story? Do they like a light on? Do you prefer their door open or closed?	
What do you want the children to wear for outdoor play? For naptime? For bedtime? Where do I put the dirty clothing?	
Is there any equipment I might be using to take care of the children that you want to show me?	
Are there any special care needs for the children? Tutoring? Music practice? Sports practice? Faith practices?	

Business Basics

What is the date and beginning and ending time of the job?	
What rules do you want me to observe in your home? Can I use the TV, radio, computer, or phone? Am I allowed to do homework? May I fix a snack?	
I usually charge $_____ for my hourly rate. Is that okay with you? Will you be paying by cash or check?	

LEADERSHIP:
SHINING STARS FOR SAFE AND RESPONSIBLE BABYSITTING

● ● ●

The Babysitter as Leader and Role Model

Parents and guardians rely on you to keep their children safe while they are away. You are a leader because children look to you as the responsible person in charge. A leader makes thoughtful decisions and knows how to use his or her skills.

You are also a role model for the children in your care. Young children watch what you do and how you handle yourself in different situations. They are likely to act in the same way you do.

As a babysitter, you can be a good leader and role model by —

◆ Keeping yourself and the children safe.

◆ Communicating well with both the children and the parents or guardians.

◆ Making decisions carefully.

◆ Guiding the children's behavior appropriately.

◆ Respecting the diversity of different people and households.

◆ Using tools that can help you do a better job, such as the Babysitter's Handbook and the Safety and First Aid Kit.

◆ Evaluating yourself after each job.

Respecting House Rules

Before accepting a babysitting job, use the Family Interview Form, p.5–7, to learn as much as you can from the parents or guardians about their children and about house rules. The parents or guardians can tell you what to expect and how they handle certain situations. The children will be happier and will feel more secure if you follow their usual routines. This is especially comforting for children who become upset when their parents or guardians are away from home.

Reporting to the Parents or Guardians

When the parents or guardians return home, take a few minutes to tell them how their children acted. Use the Babysitter's Report Record, p. 22–23.

Follow these guidelines:

◆ *Be specific.* Tell them exactly what happened, and be sure to report if anything out of the ordinary occurred.

◆ *Be complete.* Report anything unusual that happened (for example, a young child who usually goes to sleep easily cried when getting ready for bed).

◆ *Be positive.* Tell them good things about their children.

◆ *Be honest.* Tell them if a child misbehaved or if you had a problem with anything.

◆ *Be polite.* Talk to the parents or guardians with courtesy and respect.

Respecting Diversity (Differences)

People are alike in many ways. In other ways, people are very different. These differences are called "diversity." Diversity is a good thing. Without diversity, everyone would be exactly the same, and that would make the world a very boring place. Accept each infant or child as someone special. You may find that the **infants** or children you babysit are diverse in some ways:

◆ *Age and development.* Children change as they get older. An older child does not play the same as an infant because of differences in development.

> How can I do the best job?

9

◆ **Developmental stages** is the phrase for how typical infants and children grow and what they can do at certain ages. The developmental stages described later in this lesson are guidelines, not rules. Many infants and children act in different ways even at the same ages and stages.

◆ *Gender.* Boys and girls may act the same way and do the same things even though they are physically different. Both boys and girls may enjoy sports, reading, playing games, and watching television.

◆ *Individual differences.* Infants and children can vary in their responses to the same situation. Nothing ever seems to bother some infants or children, while others cry very easily.

◆ *Cultural differences.* You may babysit for an infant or child whose family is from a different country or culture. The family may speak with an accent, look different, or dress differently than you. You can learn a lot from these families — all about new foods, customs, and holidays. This is also a fun way to learn new words. Respect all of these differences.

◆ *Religious beliefs.* You may care for children with religious beliefs different from your own. Parents may ask you, "Make sure Johnnie says his prayers" or "Help Sarah light a Hanukkah candle." Respect each family's religion.

◆ *Family members.* You may care for infants or children living with one parent, with a stepparent or guardian, or with other relatives who are not the infant or child's parents. Accept all family members.

◆ *Family income.* All families do not have the same amount of money to spend. Infants and children have different kinds of toys and clothes. Give the same good care to all infants and children, no matter how much the family spends on clothes, toys, food, and other things.

Making Decisions

In many problem situations, you will know what to do if you follow the guidelines in this handbook. For example, if an infant or child has a cut that needs bandaging, follow the steps for first aid in the First Aid Action Plans. In other situations, you will have to make decisions on your own, such as what to do when an infant or child is acting up. In these situations, use the FIND model to help you decide what to do.

FIND Decision-Making Model

Step 1: Figure out the problem

◆ What do you have to decide?

◆ Make sure you focus on the exact problem that is causing trouble.

Step 2: Identify solutions

◆ What are your choices?

◆ Think about all possible ways you could solve the problem.

Step 3: Name the pros and cons of each choice

◆ Think about the pros and cons of each way to solve the problem.

Step 4: Decide which is the best choice, then act on it

◆ Decide which is the best solution.

Use the FIND model to help make the best possible decision!

FiND DECiSiON-MAKiNG MODEL ACTiViTY

● ● ●

Your instructor will tell you how to fill
out this page during class.

Figure

out the prob-
lem. "What do
I need to
decide?"

identify

solutions. "What
are my choices of
what to do?"

Name

the pros and cons
of each choice.
"What are the
advantages and
disadvantages of
each way to solve
the problem?"

Decide

which is the
best choice, then
act on it. "What
will I do now?"

FIND DECISION-MAKING MODEL ACTIVITY PAGE

• • •

I am confident with my decision!

? ? ? ? ? ? ? ? ?

F

i

N

D

Use the FIND model to help make the best possible decision!

Common Babysitting Problems: Using the FIND Model to Decide What to Do

Babysitters often encounter specific kinds of problems with children in their care, especially problems involving meals, homework or chores, TV or video games, and bedtime. Below are common babysitting problems with some possible solutions. Think about which solutions would work best for you and why. What are some other solutions you could use while on the job? Practice using the FIND model to decide what to do.

Problem: **Child refuses to eat dinner.**

Some possible FIND solutions:

◆ If you can, give the child choices, such as carrots or green beans, macaroni and cheese or spaghetti.

◆ If the child becomes hungry later on, offer the dinner he or she first refused.

◆ Explain to the child that if he or she won't eat dinner, he or she will not get any snacks for the rest of the evening.

Problem: **Child refuses to pick up toys.**

Some possible FIND solutions:

◆ Do not let the child get out new toys until the other toys are put away.

◆ Offer to help the child put away the toys.

◆ Make cleanup interesting. Suggest that the child put toys away by color; start with the child's favorite color.

Problem: **Child refuses to go to bed.**

Some possible FIND solutions:

◆ Prepare the child for bed ahead of time by saying it's time for bed right after the present activity is over.

◆ Make bedtime pleasant by reading the child a story or playing soft music.

◆ If the child still won't go to bed, say you will have to report this to the parents or guardians.

Problem: **Child refuses to do homework.**

Some possible FIND solutions:

◆ Do not let the child talk on the phone, watch television, or do anything else until the homework is complete.

◆ Ask the child what he or she is studying in school. Ask to see the homework. Then guide him or her into doing the homework one step at a time. Show your interest, and praise the child for doing the homework.

Problem: **Infant will not stop crying.**

Some possible FIND solutions:

◆ Burp the infant.

◆ Offer a bottle, and see if the infant will take it.

◆ Check to see if the infant needs to have his or her diaper changed.

◆ Check to see if the infant's clothing is tight or uncomfortable.

◆ Pick up the infant, and hold and comfort him or her.

AGES AND STAGES

Infant (Newborn to 12 Months)

◆ Reaches for objects

◆ Lifts chest off ground, supported by arms

◆ Smiles and laughs

◆ Rolls over

◆ Picks up and holds small objects

◆ Explores by putting things in mouth

◆ Supports own head (at about 6 months old)

◆ "Talks" baby talk or babbles (ma-ma, ba-ba, da-da, na-na)

◆ Crawls

◆ Acts shy with new people

◆ Gets into a sitting position (at about 6 to 8 months old)

◆ Waves and plays games like peekaboo

◆ Pulls self up to a standing position (at about 9 to 12 months old)

◆ Stands alone for a second or two (at about 10 to 12 months old)

◆ Moves around by holding on to furniture for support: "cruising" (at about 9 to 12 months old)

◆ Claps hands

◆ Begins to take first steps

Toddler (1 to 3 Years)

◆ Drinks from a cup

◆ Walks well (younger toddler); runs well (older toddler)

◆ Feeds self (with hands first and then with small spoon and fork)

◆ Learns to talk (from single words to simple sentences; using over 50 words by age 2)

◆ Becomes easily frustrated

◆ Is physically very active and busy

◆ Walks up steps, but needs help to be safe on steps (by about 19 months)

◆ Walks down steps, but needs help to be safe on steps (by about 2 years old)

◆ Builds with blocks

◆ Imitates simple adult activities (such as using a hairbrush or trying to open the door with keys)

◆ Brushes teeth (usually needs help until about 2½ years old)

◆ Dresses self (with lots of supervision and help)

◆ Washes and dries hands (if able to reach the sink safely)

◆ Recognizes and names favorite people and objects

Preschooler (3 to 5 Years)

◆ Balances on one foot, hops (tries to roller-skate by age 5)

◆ Moves constantly (can climb fences by age 5)

◆ Catches bouncing ball (can throw a ball overhand by age 4)

◆ Rides a tricycle (can ride bike with training wheels by age 4)

◆ Uses hands more (older child can do simple puzzles)

◆ Presses buttons on phone keypad

◆ Takes off shoes, socks, pants; puts on simple clothes (can dress, lace shoes, and undress with supervision by age 4)

◆ Has more control of own toilet routine (may wear diaper or training pants at night)

◆ Washes hands and face (can do normal daily hygiene by age 5, but a little clumsy)

◆ Talks well and asks a lot of questions; memory improving

School-Aged Child (5 to 8 Years)

◆ Arms and legs growing and becoming more coordinated (enjoys playing sports, jumping rope, and skipping games by age 6 to 7)

◆ Weight and height increasing (faster for boys up to 9 years old)

◆ Dresses, bathes, and eats by self with supervision

◆ Loses baby teeth; permanent teeth coming in

◆ Begins to follow rules and enjoys games with rules

◆ Tells difference between real and make-believe (begins to think out problems by age 7)

◆ Uses hands to work with tools (paintbrushes, computers, needle and thread)

◆ Makes first attempts at learning to play music

◆ Learns to tell time

◆ Becomes more independent and self-reliant

◆ May enjoy collecting things as a hobby (by age 8)

Infants and children are individuals. Many infants and children act in different ways, even if they are at the same ages and development stages!

Being a Good Communicator with Children

Knowing how to talk to and how to listen to children will make you a good communicator.

Keep It Simple
◆ Use short sentences and simple words to avoid confusing children.

Keep It Positive
◆ Tell children what you want them to do instead of what you want them not to do. For example, say, "Please put your plate in the sink" instead of "Don't leave your plate on the table."

Be Specific
◆ Tell children exactly what you like or don't like about what they are doing. For example, say, "I like it when you pick up your toys" rather than "You're a good girl."

Show Courtesy and Respect
◆ Say "please" and "thank you." Children will copy this behavior.

◆ Do not call children names. Calling children "stupid" or "bad" does not explain to them what they did wrong. Name-calling may also make children angry and cause hurt feelings.

Stay Calm
◆ Talk in a calm voice when disciplining, even if you are upset or angry. If a child screams or carries on, say, "I can't understand you when you yell." Never shake an infant.

Show You Are Listening
◆ If you can't do what the child wants right away, let the child know that you are listening and have heard his or her feelings. For example, if a child wants to go to the park and you need to ask his or her mother first, explain this to him or her. Children will not feel ignored if you show them you are listening.

Helping Children Behave

Children often need help learning how to control their behavior and how to express themselves. When a child is misbehaving, for example, you can use different ways to encourage the child to stop or change the misbehavior.

When a child misbehaves, there are three kinds of things you can do:

◆ Do nothing.

◆ Say something.

◆ Physically do something.

Each of these methods works best in different situations.

◆ Doing nothing means you ignore the child's misbehavior. Doing nothing is a method you can use when a child is misbehaving to get your attention. *Example:* If a child throws a temper tantrum but is not hurting himself or herself or anyone else, you can ignore the behavior.

◆ Saying something means you tell the child what to do or what not to do. Saying something is a method you will use to solve most common babysitting problems. *Example:* A child is playing with a water pistol in the house. You explain that water pistols are outside toys. You give the child a choice of playing with something else or taking the water pistol outside.

◆ Physically doing something means you physically stop the child from misbehaving. Physically stop the child when the child's behavior is a physical threat to himself or herself or to others. *Examples:* If the child tries to hit you, firmly grasp the child's arm before he or she can hit you and say, "I won't let you hit me. If you're angry, tell me with words." If the child is about to throw a toy, take the toy away.

Correcting the Behavior without Criticizing the Child

Children need to know that you won't stop liking them if they misbehave. Make sure children know that you are unhappy with what they did, rather than with them.

GOLD MEDAL PERFORMANCE CHECKOFF

Your instructor will tell you how to fill out this page during class.

FIND Decision-Making Model

Did the babysitter in the role play—

☐ Figure out exactly what the problem was?

☐ Identify choices for possible solutions?

☐ Name the pros and cons of each choice?

☐ Decide on a specific solution?

Communication Skills of Babysitter

Did the babysitter in the role play use statements that were—

☐ Simple and clear?

☐ Positive?

☐ Specific?

☐ Courteous and respectful?

Did the babysitter in the role play—

☐ Use a calm voice?

☐ Acknowledge the child's feelings?

☐ Listen and respond to the child?

Helping Children Behave
Did the babysitter in the role play—

☐ Explain limits and rules?

☐ Consider the child's developmental stage?

☐ Give positive feedback?

☐ Use corrective feedback for undesired behavior?

☐ Correct misbehavior appropriately by doing nothing, saying something, or physically doing something?

☐ Correct misbehavior in a positive way?

BABYSITTER'S REPORT RECORD
• • •

1. Household Rules and Discipline

a. I noticed these good behaviors:

_____

b. I used the discipline technique you asked me to use when—

_____

2. Safety

a. We received the following phone calls and visitors:

Date and time	Name	Reason for calling or visiting	Phone number to reach the caller or visitor

b. The following accidents and illnesses happened while you were gone:

Date and time	What happened	What I Did	What the child did

3. Play

    a. We played with the following games and toys:

    _____

    b. I noticed these good behaviors while we were playing:

    _____

    _____

4. Basic Care

    a. We ate the following foods:

    _____

    b. _____ had naptime/went to

    bed at_____.

    _____had naptime/went to bed

    at_____.

    c. I changed the diaper/helped with toileting _____ times, and
    I noticed _____

    _____.

    I changed the diaper/helped with toileting _____ times and I
    noticed _____

    _____.

5. Other Comments

_____

_____

_____

_____

STOP: THINK SAFETY!

● ● ●

Safety First

As a babysitter, your biggest responsibility is to keep infants and children safe while their parents or guardians are away. To prevent injuries, watch out for safety-related problems. If you recognize a problem, try to remove the safety-related problem or limit the chance of an injury or illness happening.

● ●

Inside and around the home, think about how you can prevent—

◆ Choking, suffocation, **and** strangulation.

◆ **Drowning.**

◆ **Falls.**

◆ **Burns.**

◆ **Fires.**

◆ **Poisoning.**

◆ **Wounds.**

◆ Riding toy/vehicle injuries.

◆ **Bites** and stings.

◆ Illness.

◆ Safety-related problems in special environments.

● ●

Be a Good Role Model

◆ Children see how you act and may imitate you.

◆ Follow the parents' or guardians' guidelines for safe play.

◆ Wash your hands, and keep food areas clean.

◆ Be aware of possible safety-related problems wherever you are.

- Know how to use the **First Aid Action Plans** if an injury or illness occurs.
- Wear proper protective gear when participating in outdoor activities with children, such as biking or roller blading.

● ●

Preventing Injuries and Illnesses

- *Recognize* the safety-related problem.
- *Remove* the safety-related problem if it is safe to do so.
- *Limit* the safety-related problem if you can't remove it.
- *Give* care if an emergency does occur.

● ●

Recognize the Safety-Related Problem

- Use your Family Interview Form, pp. 5–7, and the Safety Inspection Checklist, pp. 45–46, to learn about any safety-related problems around the home.
- Check the home and area around it before starting the job.
- Ask the parents or guardians about special safety equipment, such as childproof locks or latches for drawers, doors, windows, and medicine cabinets; smoke detectors; and security devices.
- Stay alert. Supervise children closely to prevent injuries while you are on the job.
- Check that electrical outlets have safety covers.
- Make sure the parents or guardians teach you about any equipment for children with special needs. Make sure you have an opportunity to practice with it before the parents or guardians leave.
- Carry the Babysitter's Handbook in the *American Red Cross Safety and First Aid Kit* to your babysitting jobs. The Kit contains first aid supplies.
- Use your Babysitter's Report Record, pp. 22–23, to let the parents or guardians know about any safety-related problems.

Remove the Safety-Related Problem

◆ Pick up lint, buttons, and any small objects from the floor to avoid choking problems.

◆ Ask the parents or guardians to lock up or remove anything that could poison a child.

◆ Keep toys with small parts away from young children.

◆ Put away broken toys or toys with sharp edges.

◆ Keep cords or strings longer than 3 inches away from infants and small children.

◆ Shut doors to bathrooms and other rooms where a child could get hurt.

● ●

Limit the Safety-Related Problem

◆ Teach safety in a positive way; use "do" instead of "don't."

◆ Give children safe and real choices.

◆ Know the Family Fire Escape Plan.

◆ Teach and model good health practices, such as handwashing.

Give Care

◆ Provide care if an emergency occurs. Refer to the First Aid Action Plans, which begin on p. 107.

I always refer to my First Aid Action Plans in case of an Emergency!

CHOKING, SUFFOCATION, AND STRANGULATION ● ● ●

Choking, suffocation, and strangulation are emergencies in which an infant or child cannot cough, speak, cry, or breathe because the airway is partly or completely blocked. Note: Be aware and especially careful with infants and toddlers. They put things in their mouths and can easily choke.

Recognize the Safety-Related Problem

◆ Look around the home and play areas for small objects that could cause choking.

● ●

Remove the Safety-Related Problem

◆ Keep infants and children away from choking and suffocation dangers like plastic bags; balloons; small balls, marbles, and toys intended for older children; disposable gloves; beads; pebbles; buttons; caps; hairpins; and jewelry. Remove small objects from the crib.

◆ Remove objects that can wrap around or cover the face, such as pillows, cushions, and beanbags.

◆ Keep cords on blinds and draperies out of reach to prevent strangulation. Never hang a diaper bag on the crib.

◆ Make sure clothing does not have drawstrings longer than 3 inches. Sleepwear should not have drawstrings at all.

◆ Avoid foods that can be dangerous for infants and toddlers:

- Small food items like raisins, popcorn, nuts, hard candy, grapes, snack chips, hot dog slices, raw vegetables, and marshmallows

- Large food items that break into small pieces: teething biscuits and cookies

Limit the Safety-Related Problem

◆ Always have children sit when eating.

◆ Do not let children walk or run, play, or talk with food in their mouths.

◆ Cut food into small pieces.

◆ Encourage children to take small bites and chew thoroughly.

Give Care

◆ If choking does occur, see the First Aid Action Plans for Choking, pp. 118–122.

DROWNING

Drowning is death by suffocation when submerged in water.

Recognize the Safety-Related Problem

◆ Understand that an infant or toddler can drown in any water, even in a few inches of water.

◆ Do not babysit around pools or other water if you are not trained in water safety and there are no trained lifeguards on duty.

Remove the Safety-Related Problem

◆ Empty wading pools when not in use.

◆ Keep pool gates locked.

Limit the Safety-Related Problem

◆ Never leave a child alone, even for a moment, in a bathtub or near any water, even a bucket with a small amount of water.

◆ Keep bathroom doors closed and toilet lids down.

◆ Bath an infant or child only if you have been taught to do so and you have the approval of the parents or guardians.

◆ Be sure lifeguards are on duty if you take children swimming. Even at a guarded facility, supervision is your responsibility.

◆ Never trust water flotation devices to prevent drowning.

Give Care

◆ If a drowning does occur, see the First Aid Action Plans for Rescue Breathing, Child, pp.134–135, and Rescue Breathing, Infant, pp. 135–136.

FALLS

Recognize the Safety-Related Problem

◆ Look for anything that could cause an infant or toddler to trip or fall from a height.

Remove the Safety-Related Problem

◆ Keep toys, books, shoes, and clutter off the stairs.

◆ Keep the play area free of extra toys.

◆ Keep electric cords away from doors and traffic paths.

Limit the Safety-Related Problem

◆ Use safety gates and closed doors to keep children from stairs; make the stairways off-limits.

◆ Keep safety rails or sides up on cribs and beds.

◆ NEVER leave an infant alone in a high chair or on a changing table or other high surface.

◆ Make sure you have access to a flashlight.

◆ Put the infant on the floor to play, away from stairs and doors.

◆ Keep doors, windows, fences, and gates locked.

Give Care

◆ If a fall does occur, see the First Aid Action Plans, beginning on p. 107, to care for the appropriate injury.

BURNS

Recognize the Safety-Related Problem

◆ Always be aware that a child can be burned by anything that is hot, including food, bathwater, heaters, and stoves or ovens.

Remove the Safety-Related Problem

◆ Keep all hot liquids away from infants and children.

◆ Test the temperature of hot foods before feeding infants and children.

◆ Keep children away from all sources of heat; check rooms carefully for all potential burn risks.

Limit the Safety-Related Problem

◆ Turn pot handles toward the back of the stove, out of the reach of children.

◆ Keep children from playing with safety covers on electrical outlets.

◆ Never hold a child and cook at the same time.

◆ Always use hot pads or oven mitts to remove pots and pans from the stove or oven. Always place these hot items out the reach of children.

◆ Make sure you and the children use sunscreen for outdoor activities, stay out of direct sun, or wear protective clothing (a hat, a long-sleeved shirt, and sunglasses).

Give Care

◆ If a burn does occur, see the First Aid Action Plan for Burns, p. 114–115.

FiRE

Recognize the Safety-Related Problem

◆ Be watchful around any hot item, such as stoves, heaters, fire-places, and grills.

Remove the Safety-Related Problem

◆ Keep toys, curtains, and similar things away from any hot item.

◆ Keep matches and lighters away from children.

◆ Keep all electrical equipment away from water.

Limit the Safety-Related Problem

◆ Talk to parents or guardians about a Family Fire Escape Plan.

◆ Know how to use the fire extinguisher and where it is kept.

◆ Teach children to Stop, Drop, and Roll if their clothing catches on fire.

◆ Teach children to crawl low under smoke and to test for hot doors.

If Fire Occurs

◆ Get yourself and the children out, and don't return to a burning building. Your job is to protect the children and yourself, not their belongings.

POISONING

Recognize the Safety-Related Problem

◆ Know what items can be poisonous to infants and children.

Remove the Safety-Related Problem

◆ Keep all poisons away from children, including cleaning products, polishes, and car products.

◆ Keep children away from alcohol, drugs, medicines, vitamins, makeup, and tobacco.

◆ Keep children away from houseplants or garden plants that they could put into their mouths.

◆ Keep children away from peeling paint or plaster.

Limit the Safety-Related Problem

◆ If parents ask you to give a child medicine, call medicine by its name. Do not call it "candy."

◆ Never take products out of child-resistant containers.

◆ Check for safety latches or locks on cabinets and doors.

◆ Keep children away from cabinets without locks.

Give Care

◆ Know the **Poison Control Center** phone number, or call 9-1-1, the local emergency number, or 0 for the operator.

◆ If a poisoning does occur, see the First Aid Action Plan for Poisoning, pp. 133—134.

WOUNDS

Recognize the Safety-Related Problem

◆ Check toys for sharp edges.

◆ Check the room for objects or surfaces that could cause wounds.

Remove the Safety-Related Problem

◆ Remove all sharp objects from children's reach.

◆ Ask parents or guardians to lock up dangerous things like knives, power tools, and guns.

Limit the Safety-Related Problem

◆ Keep children away from large glass doors or windows.

◆ Make sure play areas are safe.

◆ Make sure children wear the right clothing for the weather, and ask parents or guardians about the proper protective gear for outdoor activities.

◆ Supervise all play closely.

◆ Make sure children always wear shoes.

◆ Supervise play with family pets.

Give Care

◆ If a wound does occur, see the First Aid Action Plan for Bleeding, pp. 113–114.

RIDING TOY/VEHICLE INJURIES

• • •

Recognize the Safety-Related Problem

◆ Accidents with riding toys and motor vehicles can cause serious injuries.

Remove the Safety-Related Problem

◆ Don't let children ride near pools, in streets, or on steps.

◆ Don't dress children in clothes with drawstrings, cords, or other items that can catch.

Limit the Safety-Related Problem

◆ Keep children away from curbs, parked cars, and the street.

◆ Teach safety rules for crossing the street:

- Look both ways before crossing.

- Hold hands when crossing the street.

- Cross only at the crosswalk.

◆ Have children wear a helmet and other protective gear when playing on riding toys.

◆ Dress children in bright colors so they can be easily seen.

Give Care

◆ If an injury does occur, use the First Aid Action Plans to care for the appropriate type of injury.

BiTES AND STINGS

Recognize the Safety-Related Problem

◆ Know what animals and insects are common to your area and how to avoid them.

Remove the Safety-Related Problem

◆ Keep children from digging or reaching into areas where these creatures may live, such as in woodpiles, near garbage, under logs, and in leaves or brush.

Limit the Safety-Related Problem

◆ Stay away from any wild animal or pet that is acting strangely.

Give Care

◆ If a bite or sting does occur, see the First Aid Action Plans for Bites and Stings, pp. 110–113.

Recognize the Safety-Related Problem

◆ Although germs are present in most places, you can keep them from entering the body and causing illness.

Remove the Safety-Related Problem

◆ Wash your hands before preparing food and after toileting or diapering, coughing, sneezing, or blowing your nose. Always wash your hands after giving first aid.

◆ Make sure infants' and children's hands are washed before and after eating and after toileting or diapering, coughing, sneezing, or blowing their nose.

Limit the Safety-Related Problem

◆ Keep toys clean.

◆ Use tissues and cover mouth and nose when coughing and sneezing.

◆ Keep trash out of the reach of children.

◆ Refrigerate foods that can spoil.

◆ If you or the child touches a wild animal or its droppings, wash hands well.

Give Care

◆ If illness does occur, use the First Aid Action Plans for appropriate care.

Family pets are healthy, clean, and child-friendly.

FiND iT! FiX iT! REPORT iT!
● ● ●

Your instructor will tell you how to fill out this page during class.

FiND iT! FiX iT! REPORT iT! ACTIVITY PAGE

• • •

Safety-Related Problem	How to Remove It	How to Limit It

HANDWASHING FACTS
● ● ●

Diseases are spread by passing germs from one person to another. People pass germs by touching each other or by touching surfaces and items after other people have touched them with dirty hands. Handwashing is the number 1 way to prevent passing germs and spreading infectious diseases.

Babysitter's Job

Always wash your hands —
◆ Before you touch children.
◆ Before you prepare food.
◆ Before and after you eat.
◆ After changing diapers or helping a child with toileting.
◆ After using the toilet.
◆ After giving first aid.
◆ After coughing, sneezing, or blowing your nose.

Make sure children wash their hands —
◆ Before and after they eat.
◆ After they use the toilet (or after infants are diapered).
◆ After they touch objects or surfaces used by other people in public areas: for example, after they come home from the playground.
◆ Before and after they put their hands in their mouths or touch their faces.
◆ After they cough, sneeze, or blow their noses.
◆ After they touch or handle insects or pets.

TEACHING HANDWASHING SKILLS

1 Remove watches and jewelry.

2 Wash for about 20 seconds. Use soap and warm running water. Scrub nails by rubbing them against the palms of your hands.

3 Rinse thoroughly.

4 Dry your hands with a paper towel.

5 Turn off the faucet using the paper towel. Throw the paper towel away.

6 Don't forget to put your watch and jewelry back on.

SAFETY-RELATED PROBLEMS IN SPECIAL ENVIRONMENTS
● ● ●

Parks and Outdoors

Recognize the Safety-Related Problem

◆ Check the nearby area for rough spots, holes, and any objects that could trip a child.

◆ Look for poisonous plants and plants with thorns, stickers, low roots, roots that stick up, or low branches that could cause scratches.

◆ Check for trash, broken glass, needles, broken cement, animal droppings, sewage, and shiny objects, like opened aluminum cans, that can cut.

◆ Check that restrooms are clean and safe for children.

◆ Inspect play equipment for good condition, and look for openings or railings that could trap a child's hands, head, or feet (any space larger than the width of a soda can is unsafe).

◆ Check for sand, wood chips, or rubber matting under play equipment to cushion a child's fall.

◆ Check that the sand in sandboxes is clean enough for the children to play in.

◆ Look for animals loose in the area.

◆ Watch for any holes or openings a child could fall into.

◆ Look for storm drains, and keep the children away from them, especially after a rainstorm.

◆ Check for any water in the area, such as a pond or a lake.

Limit the Safety-Related Problem

◆ Keep the children away from any unsafe conditions you find.

◆ Dress the children and yourself appropriately.

◆ Don't dress the children in garments that could catch on playground equipment.

Give Care

◆ Make sure you have coins for an emergency telephone call from a pay phone in case an injury occurs. You do not need to pay to call 9-1-1 or 0. A cellular phone comes in handy for emergencies.

BEING PREPARED FOR ENVIRONMENTAL EMERGENCIES
● ● ●

Check your Family Interview Form, pp. 5–7, for the parents' or guardians' instructions in case of an emergency.

Violence or Crime

◆ Be aware of your surroundings and what is going on around you.

◆ Avoid wearing or doing anything that would get you noticed.

◆ Know how to open security bars or doors and how to get out of the house or apartment building.

◆ If you hear gunfire, hit the ground and wait for 20 to 30 minutes before leaving cover; call the police or 9-1-1 as soon as the scene is safe.

◆ If it looks as if the home has been broken into when you return from an outing, do not enter. Take the children to a safe area, such as a designated neighbor, local business, or police station. Your job is to protect yourself and the children, not their belongings.

Electrical Storms

◆ If you are outside, go inside or seek shelter.

◆ Do not shower, bathe, or touch water.

◆ Know where flashlights and extra batteries are kept.

◆ Turn off electrical appliances, such as the TV.

◆ Stay off the phone during storms.

◆ Comfort and keep track of the children during storms and power outages.

◆ In case of fire, know where fire stairs, fire exits, and escape ladders are in high-rise buildings and how to use them.

◆ Know where fire alarms and smoke detectors are located.

◆ Know the location of fire extinguishers and how to use them.

Floods, Earthquakes, Tornadoes, Winter Storms, and Hurricanes

◆ Know where the disaster supplies kit is kept and what's in it.

◆ Listen to the radio or TV for instructions on what to do and where to go.

◆ Know where to take the children for shelter, especially if you are in a mobile home.

◆ Know where and how to turn off the power.

◆ During winter storms, keep children inside and warm.

SAFETY INSPECTION CHECKLIST – CHECK IT OUT! •••

☐ **The emergency phone list has been filled out and is posted**

_____
_____
_____
_____.

☐ **The first aid kit is stored**

_____
_____
_____
_____.

☐ **The fire extinguisher is located**

_____
_____
_____
_____.

☐ **Flashlights are located**

_____
_____
_____
_____.

☐ **The children are not allowed in**

_____
_____
_____.

(Examples include garage, basement, office)

To Prevent Wounds

- [ ] Guns, knives, power tools, razor blades, scissors, and other objects that can cause injury are stored in locked cabinets or storage areas.

To Prevent Falls

- [ ] Safety gates are installed at all open stairways.
- [ ] Windows and balcony doors have childproof latches.
- [ ] Balconies have protective barriers to prevent children from slipping through bars.
- [ ] The home is free of clutter on the floors and especially on or near stairways.

To Prevent Poisoning

- [ ] Potential poisons like detergents, polishes, pesticides, plant fertilizer, shampoo, and cosmetics are stored in locked cabinets.
- [ ] Houseplants are kept out of reach.
- [ ] Medicine is kept in a locked storage place that children can't reach.

To Prevent Burns

- [ ] Safety covers are placed on all unused electrical outlets.
- [ ] Loose cords are secured and out of the way. Multicord or octopus plugs are not used. (They may overheat and cause fires.)
- [ ] At least one approved smoke detector is installed and operating near the sleeping area.

- [ ] Space heaters are placed out of the reach of children and away from curtains.
- [ ] **Flammable** liquids are securely stored in their original containers.
- [ ] Matches and lighters are stored out of the reach of children.
- [ ] Garbage and recycling materials are stored in covered containers.
- [ ] The children in the house know and have practiced a Family Fire Escape Plan.

To Prevent Drowning

- [ ] Swimming pools and hot tubs are completely enclosed with a barrier, such as a locked fence or cover.
- [ ] Wading pools are emptied when not in use.
- [ ] The toilet seat and lid are kept down when not in use.
- [ ] The bathroom door is kept closed.

To Prevent Choking and Suffocation

- [ ] The toy box has ventilation holes, and if it has a lid, it is a lightweight removable lid, a sliding door or panel, or a hinged lid with a support to hold it open.
- [ ] The crib mattress fits the side of the crib snugly and toys, blankets, and pillows are removed from the crib.
- [ ] Small objects are kept out of children's reach.

SAFE PLAY

Play It Safe!

Keep children safe during play by supervising them at all times. While you play with the children, watch how they respond to learn what activities they like best and how they want to play.

◆ Follow the family's rules for play. (See the Family Interview Form, pp. 5–7.)

◆ Choose the right toys and games for each child, based on his or her developmental stage and personal preferences. Safety depends on the right toy and activity at the right age.

◆ Actively play with the children—don't just watch from the sidelines.

Why should you play with the children?

◆ It is easy to supervise the children during play and to remove any safety-related problems from the area.

◆ Playing allows you to teach and praise positive behaviors, as well as control any behavior problems.

◆ Playing is fun and helps you feel you've done a good job as a babysitter.

How can you help children play?

◆ Respect their likes and dislikes in choosing toys and games.

◆ Be truly interested and involved in their play.

Be a Good Role Model

◆ Be aware of safety in all activities.

◆ Wash your hands, and keep toys and play areas clean.

◆ Cheerfully resolve any problems that arise during play.

◆ Enjoy playing with the children.

I even wash my paws!

Why Should Children Play?

◆ Playing helps children develop physically. This includes running, jumping, dancing, putting beads on a string, and coloring.

◆ Playing helps children develop mentally. Learning rhymes, singing songs, doing puzzles, sorting and naming things, counting, and reading—all of these help children grow.

◆ Playing helps children understand and control their emotions. This may involve banging a drum, playacting, imagining, asking "what if" questions, or playing games with others.

◆ Playing helps children develop socially. Pretending to be someone else, acting out a story, playing team sports, playing an instrument in a band, taking turns jumping rope, and playing board games with others—all of these give children stronger social skills.

How Do Children Play?

Children play in different ways as they develop and grow older. You will play in different ways with children at different ages and developmental stages.

◆ Infants first play by themselves.

◆ Older infants play while watching others, but they rarely interact directly with others.

◆ Toddlers may play alongside other toddlers, but they rarely share and interact with one another.

◆ As toddlers develop into preschoolers, they play side by side and begin interacting and sharing.

◆ Preschoolers enjoy interacting with one another. Games like Duck Duck Goose have simple rules and offer lots of opportunity for interaction. Sometimes, preschoolers want to make up their own rules.

◆ School-aged children learn to play in an organized way. They take on roles, understand having a leader, and can play as a team. Rules are very important to them.

CREATE PLAY

Your instructor will tell you how to fill out this page during class.

Instructions

As a group, fill in your assigned column. When the other two groups report back, fill in the other two columns.

	Paper	5 Senses	Household Items
Infants	Peekaboo		
Toddlers		Name colors of common objects	
Preschoolers	Make a paper hat		
School-Aged Children			Use paper bags and crayons to make puppets

SAFETY AND TOYS

Choose the toys that are right for each child. Here are some suggestions.

Infants (Newborn to 6 Months)
Toys

- Soft mobiles
- Rattles
- Soft fabric swatches
- Stuffed animals

Infants (6 Months to 1 Year)
Toys

- Large colored blocks made of rubber or soft material
- Large nesting boxes or cups
- Squeaky toys or bells
- Large balls
- Pots and pans
- Wooden spoons and plastic bowls
- Simple picture books, cloth books
- Push-pull toys
- Teething toys

Activities

- Music of different types
- Reading
- Rhymes
- Hand games like peekaboo or finger play
- Looking at self in mirror

* No toy should be less than 1¼ inches in diameter

1¼

For a free copy of the publication, "Which Toy for Which Child: Ages Birth through 5," write for item #285, U.S. Consumer Product Safety Commission, Washington, DC 20207. More safety information is available over the Internet at "http://www.cpsc.gov" or by calling the Consumer Product Safety Commission's toll-free hotline, 1-800-638-2772.

Toddlers (1 to 3 Years)
Toys

- Large beads (larger than 1¼ inches in diameter) to string together
- Building blocks, buildings
- Large plastic toy people and animals
- Action toys like telephones, trains, planes, cars, and trucks
- Simple puzzles with knobs
- Puppets
- Large balls, cardboard boxes
- Books

- Drums, xylophone, other musical toys
- Pail and shovel
- Riding toys

Activities

- Reading
- Coloring and painting
- Music, dancing, singing
- Sand and water play
- Imaginative play
- Storytelling

Preschoolers (3 to 5 Years)
Toys

- Playground equipment: seesaw, swings, slides, climbing structures
- Simple board games
- Storybooks
- Balls
- Musical instruments
- Dolls and props for pretend play— cooking, cleaning, carpentry
- Skates, wagons, tricycles
- Large-piece puzzles
- Sand and water play

Activities

- Physically active games—hide-and-seek, follow the leader
- Arts and crafts

School-Aged Children (5 to 8 Years)
Toys

- Board games
- Items related to hobbies or collections—stickers, rocks, or miniature cars
- Electronic games
- Fashion and action dolls

Activities

- Reading and storytelling
- Hobbies of all kinds:
  Sewing
  Woodworking
  Gardening
- Sports
- Music and dancing
- Arts and crafts

Have enough toys for all your toddlers, and they'll play side by side.

TOY BOX JUMBLE

Children play safely with different toys at different ages. On the grid below, you will find 12 toys or activities appropriate for infants, toddlers, preschoolers, or school-aged children. Words could be horizontal, vertical, diagonal, or backward. Circle the 12 toys or activities. Then, after thinking about who could safely enjoy playing with that toy or activity, put it in the appropriate toy box by writing the word in the box. Think carefully! A few of the toys or activities might go into more than one toy box.

Toys and Activities:
Checkers, duck duck goose, mobile, finger paints, tricycle, rattle, skateboard, teething ring, books, stacking rings, peekaboo, basketball

E	E	H	H	S	T	N	I	A	P	R	E	G	N	I	F	G	A	B	O
A	A	Z	R	S	S	T	T	Y	L	E	P	P	Q	B	N	M	M	T	B
N	R	R	C	A	N	A	R	C	T	R	I	C	Y	C	L	E	O	H	E
T	J	A	T	T	U	V	H	O	P	G	H	B	E	E	T	J	O	L	N
K	S	T	E	E	T	H	I	N	G	R	I	N	G	B	B	G	C	R	T
L	A	T	D	E	M	C	C	R	S	R	G	B	J	O	D	D	T	D	B
B	I	L	D	N	A	H	H	S	N	T	C	I	I	O	O	S	E	A	D
C	J	E	S	S	E	S	O	O	G	K	C	U	D	K	C	U	D	V	E
S	R	H	E	C	L	H	P	Q	Q	E	I	Q	R	S	E	S	S	V	L
Q	P	H	K	O	O	L	K	L	L	H	O	G	Q	D	A	A	B	S	I
C	K	E	O	B	S	T	A	C	K	I	N	G	R	I	N	G	S	N	B
T	R	P	C	L	H	K	Z	B	Y	Z	M	N	O	P	N	S	S	T	O
S	T	C	C	N	M	J	K	U	T	C	A	F	F	P	K	E	D	K	M
L	Y	E	D	M	D	R	A	O	B	E	T	A	K	S	F	F	O	A	L
R	L	P	E	E	K	A	B	O	O	C	K	O	G	F	F	O	N	M	L
J	E	P	T	M	H	N	F	F	P	C	W	S	M	M	B	I	P	V	K
O	F	G	O	M	E	L	F	G	B	D	W	U	A	T	T	I	Q	J	V
H	C	O	M	M	L	E	A	A	B	N	X	N	S	B	R	A	L	A	K
N	Q	S	P	J	M	S	S	T	O	R	B	O	T	U	P	A	N	K	A

TOY BOX GAME PAGE

Infant's Toy Box

TOYS

Toddler's Toy Box

Toys

Preschooler's Toy Box

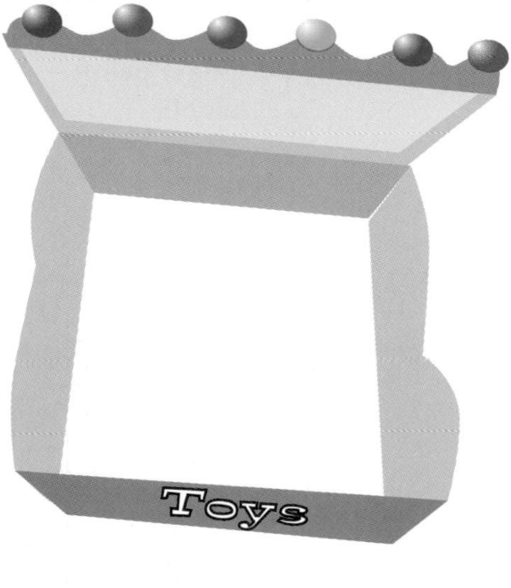

Toys

School-Aged Toy Box

Toys

E	E	H	H	S	T	N	I	A	P	R	E	G	N	I	F	G	A	B	O
A	A	Z	R	S	S	T	T	Y	L	E	P	P	Q	B	N	M	M	T	B
N	R	R	C	A	N	A	R	C	T	R	I	C	Y	C	L	E	O	H	E
T	J	A	T	T	U	V	H	O	P	G	H	B	E	E	T	J	O	L	N
K	S	T	E	E	T	H	I	N	G	R	I	N	G	B	B	G	C	R	T
L	A	T	D	E	M	C	C	R	S	R	G	B	J	O	D	D	T	D	B
B	I	L	D	N	A	H	H	S	N	T	C	I	I	O	O	S	E	A	D
C	J	E	S	S	E	S	O	O	G	K	C	U	D	K	C	U	D	V	E
S	R	H	E	C	L	H	P	Q	Q	E	I	Q	R	S	E	S	S	V	L
Q	P	H	K	O	O	L	K	L	L	H	O	G	Q	D	A	A	B	S	I
C	K	E	O	B	S	T	A	C	K	I	N	G	R	I	N	G	S	N	B
T	R	P	C	L	H	K	Z	B	Y	Z	M	N	O	P	N	S	S	T	O
S	T	C	C	N	M	J	K	U	T	C	A	F	F	P	K	E	D	K	M
L	Y	E	D	M	D	R	A	O	B	E	T	A	K	S	F	F	O	A	L
R	L	P	E	E	K	A	B	O	O	C	K	O	G	F	F	O	N	M	L
J	E	P	T	M	H	N	F	F	P	C	W	S	M	M	B	I	P	V	K
O	F	G	O	M	E	L	F	G	B	D	W	U	A	T	T	I	Q	J	V
H	C	O	M	M	L	E	A	A	B	N	X	N	S	B	R	A	L	A	K
N	Q	S	P	J	M	S	S	T	O	R	B	O	T	U	P	A	N	K	A

teething ring
stacking ring
mobile
rattle
peek-a-boo
books

Toys

tricycle
finger paints
mobile
books

Toys

tricycle
finger paints
duck duck goose
mobile
books

Toys

checkers
finger paints
basketball
skateboard
mobile
books

Toys

BASIC CARE:
THE HEART OF
BABYSITTING
● ● ●

An Overview of Basic Care

Basic care is the heart of babysitting. Effective basic care begins with understanding the family routines for care. Routines, supplies, and equipment can vary greatly among families, so it is always important to ask parents or guardians about basic care. Babysitters should also model desirable basic care behaviors in their own activities. For example, they concentrate on eating when it is mealtime, they wash their hands before and after eating and after toileting, and they make sure they get proper rest.

● ●

Basic Care Basics

- ◆ Cleanliness and personal hygiene
- ◆ Holding
- ◆ Feeding
- ◆ Diapering and toileting
- ◆ Dressing
- ◆ Rest and sleep

I know all
the basics!

Be a Good Role Model

◆ Wash your hands after assisting with toileting and before handling food.

◆ Serve healthy snack foods.

◆ Choose calming activities for quiet times.

◆ Make sure children get enough rest.

◆ Supervise children while doing basic care.

● ●

Talking to the Parents or Guardians about Basic Care

Gather information about basic care that you will need to know before you babysit. See the Family Interview Form, pp. 5–7.

◆ You will need to know what kinds of basic care skills you will use to care for the children.

◆ Children are usually happier if you stick to their basic care routine.

Report to the parents or guardians on basic care when you finish the job. Use the Babysitter's Report Record on pp. 22–23.

Find out where basic care supplies are kept. This makes the job easier.

Watch Out for Germs

While on the job, you could come in contact with germs. Germs can be transmitted by direct contact, such as getting blood or urine in a cut on your hand; by air, when breathing in droplets in the air from someone else's cough or sneeze; by contact with an object or surface that has been in contact with a germ, such as a telephone receiver or fork and knife; or by an insect, animal, or human bite. Some germs can cause you to get a cold or the flu or expose you to common childhood diseases like chicken pox and the measles. Other germs can cause serious diseases like HIV, the virus that causes AIDS.

As a babysitter, it is highly unlikely that you will get HIV unless you have blood-to-blood contact. To stay healthy and avoid the spread of germs, wear disposable gloves when you could come into contact with blood or other **body fluids**. Families may not have gloves for you, so make sure you take them with you to the job. The *American Red Cross Safety and First Aid Kit* contains disposable gloves, and you can also buy gloves at many supermarkets and drugstores.

Use a new pair of gloves—
◆ When you change a diaper.

◆ When you give first aid to someone who is bleeding.

◆ When you touch any body fluids, such as urine or **vomit**, or solid wastes like **feces**.

As a babysitter, you can catch serious diseases by handling body products like blood, urine, feces, or vomit without using gloves. Be sure to carefully remove and properly dispose of gloves after giving basic care. When you are removing gloves, be careful that you do not get any germs or dirt on yourself. Wash your hands before providing care and after disposing of your gloves when you have completed basic care.

REMOVING GLOVES

● ● ●

To Remove Dirty Gloves —

1

Pinch one glove at the wrist and remove it about two-thirds of the way, turning it inside out.

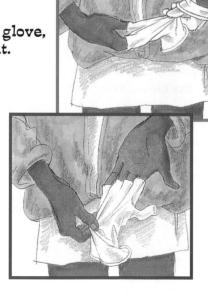

2

Pinch the second glove at the wrist.

3

Remove the second glove, turning it inside out.

4

Finish removing both gloves.

5

Discard gloves in an appropriate container.

HOLDING CHILDREN

Most children enjoy being held, although some do not. Respect individual differences.

Holding Infants

◆ Always support the head, neck, and back of infants under 6 months old.

◆ Holding the infant close to your body makes the infant feel safe and secure.

Cradle Hold

1 Support the infant's bottom and lower back with one hand.

2 Cradle the infant in your arm, and support the back with your other hand. Hold the infant's head on your arm near or at the bend of the elbow.

3 Hold the infant close to your body, with the infant's back straight and protected.

Football Hold

Use this hold when you need one hand free.

1 After lifting the infant to the cradle position, move the infant to one side so that he or she is resting at the side of your body, the infant's hip on your hip and so that you can see his or her face.

2 Using the arm on the side of your body where you are holding the infant, slide your hand with fingers spread along the infant's back and spine until you can support the head and neck in your palm.

3 Clasp your elbow to your side to tuck the infant firmly to your body.

You mean I have to carry something else!

Shoulder Hold

1 Hold the infant in an upright position so that he or she can look over your shoulder.

2 Support the head, neck, and back as shown.

Holding Toddlers

◆ If you can support their weight, toddlers like to be held and carried. Hold toddlers on your lap when giving them a bottle or a drink from a spill-proof cup or when reading to them.

◆ Toddlers may crawl off your lap if they want to play or if they see something they want to investigate.

◆ Ask toddlers to help out when you need to carry them. Toddlers can put both arms around your neck to hold on securely.

Upright Carry for Toddlers

1 Carry toddlers from one place to another in an upright position.

2 Put one arm under the toddler's bottom, and support his or her back with your other arm.

BOTTLE-FEEDING iNFANTS

● ● ●

Bottle-Feeding

◆ Ask the parents or guardians about feeding their infant. (See the Family Interview Form, pp. 5–7.) Infants and toddlers may drink milk, **formula**, fruit juices, or water from a bottle.

◆ **NEVER** heat a bottle in a microwave oven. Run the bottle under warm water to bring it to room temperature rather than microwaving.

1

Wash your hands.

2

Keep the infant safe and comfortable. Choose a safe, quiet place for feeding.

Gather supplies (bottle, nipple, bib or cloth to protect the child's clothing, towel or cloth to put over your shoulder for burping the infant). Warm and prepare the bottle as the parent or guardian directed. Gently shake the bottle to make sure it is evenly heated before giving it to the infant. Test the temperature on your wrist. It should be just about skin temperature.

4

Rest the infant or child comfortably on your lap. Be sure to keep the infant's head higher than his or her shoulders. Put the bib or cloth under the child's chin, and place a towel or cloth on your lap or shoulder to protect your clothes.

5

Give the infant the bottle. Hold the bottle for the infant, unless the infant is old enough to hold it. Carefully watch the bottle as the infant sucks so that air is not getting into the nipple.

6

Gently burp the infant when he or she has taken about one-third of the bottle. Hold the infant upright, and put his or her head on your shoulder.

7

Tap the infant gently on the back until you hear a burp. Some infants spit up a little when burped. You can also burp the infant by placing the infant on his or her stomach on your lap. Burp the infant again when finished drinking.

SPOON-FEEDING
● ● ●

1 Wash your hands.

2 Gather supplies (dish, food, infant/toddler spoon, bib). Put the food in a dish, and place the bib under the infant's or toddler's chin.

3 If the infant or toddler uses a high chair or infant seat, get the food ready before you put the child into the chair or seat. Buckle the safety belt securely.

4 Use a spoon to feed an infant strained food or cereal. Put only a small amount of food on the tip of the spoon. Infants who are just beginning to eat from a spoon may seem to be pushing the food away. Be patient and keep feeding them as long as they seem interested.

5 Wash the infant's or toddler's hands and face, and wipe up any food that was spilled.

6 Wash your hands.

64 ♥

Spoon-Feeding Older Infants and Toddlers

◆ Some parents or guardians heat food by placing the container of food into a container of hot water. If you use a microwave to heat the food, be sure to stir the food well and test the temperature before giving it to an infant or toddler. Put a small amount of food on your wrist to make sure it's cool enough. Lukewarm food won't burn the child's mouth.

◆ Don't blow on food to cool it. Let it cool by itself.

◆ Let toddlers try to feed themselves with the spoon or their hands if they want, even if they make a mess. Help toddlers as needed.

Feeding Preschoolers and School-Aged Children

◆ Follow the parents' or guardians' instructions on what and how to feed the child. (See the Family Interview Form, pp. 5–7.)

◆ Most young children eat with their fingers, although some will use a small fork or spoon. Eating is fun for most children. Don't worry if they are messy.

◆ If the child does not eat much or refuses to eat or drink, wait a few minutes and try again. If the child is playing with the food more than eating, the child has probably finished eating.

◆ Older children can feed themselves, but you will need to prepare their food. Let them pitch in by helping you set the table.

Food and Kitchen Safety

◆ Wash your hands before you prepare food.

◆ Wash raw fruits and vegetables carefully before eating them or feeding them to children.

◆ Be careful when using a microwave oven. Stir foods well after removing them from the microwave. Always test the temperature of foods and drinks before giving them to children.

◆ Never leave a child alone in a high chair — not even for a moment. Keep high chairs away from stoves and counters.

◆ If you must use the stove, put a young child in a safe play area. Use only the back burners, and turn pan handles away from the edge of the stove.

◆ Don't let children play in the kitchen.

DiAPERiNG
● ● ●

Disposable Diapers

1 Wash your hands. Wear disposable gloves.

2 Collect supplies (two diapers, disposable wipes, plastic trash bag).

3 Keep the infant or toddler safe and comfortable. Use the floor or crib, protected with a water-resistant pad, to change the infant or toddler if you are not comfortable using a changing table.

4 Never leave an infant or toddler alone on a changing table. Even newborn infants turn and squirm when they are being changed and can easily wiggle off the changing table and get hurt. Some infants or toddlers are easier to change if they have a toy to hold.

66 ♥

5 Place the infant or toddler on his or her back. Take off the dirty diaper by lifting the infant's or toddler's legs and hips high enough to slide the dirty diaper away. Fold the diaper so that the mess is on the inside. Set the dirty diaper out of the way where the infant or toddler can't reach it. Lift up the infant or toddler, and clean with wipes or a washcloth. Always clean from the front to the back, and be sure to separate the folds of the skin to remove all mess. Be gentle. When changing a boy, keep him covered with a wipe or a diaper as much as possible during the change to avoid being sprayed.

6 Use one hand to hold the infant's or toddler's feet and lift up the bottom. Use the other hand to slip the open clean diaper under the infant's or toddler's bottom. Disposable diapers fit in only one way and usually have pictures or cartoons on the front part. Use the cartoon band as a guide to put the diaper on right side up.

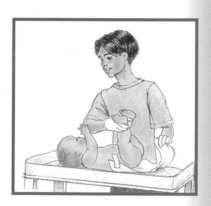

7 Fasten the diaper with the tabs. Put your fingers between the diaper and the infant or toddler so that you don't tape the diaper to him or her.

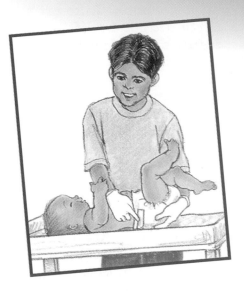

8 Properly dispose of the dirty diaper and wipes in the trash, preferably using a plastic trash bag. Make sure the changing surface is clean before removing your gloves. Put them in the plastic trash bag. (See p. 58 for how to remove gloves.) Keep one hand on the infant or toddler at all times.

9 Wash the infant's or toddler's hands, and place him or her in a safe location while you wash your own hands.

I like to keep my paws clean...

Cloth Diapers

1 Wash your hands. Wear disposable gloves.

2 Collect supplies (two diapers, two diaper pins, disposable wipes, plastic trash bag, diaper pail).

3 Fold the diaper for a boy or a girl.

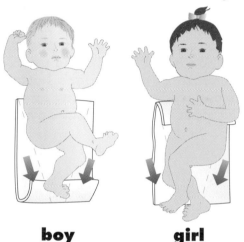

boy   **girl**

4 Remove rubber pants. Unfasten and remove the pins, keeping the pins away from the infant or toddler. You can stick the pins in a bar of soap or a pin cushion, but don't put them in your mouth.

5 Keep the infant or toddler safe and comfortable. Use the floor or crib, protected with a water-resistant pad, to change the infant or toddler if you are not comfortable using a changing table. Never leave an infant or toddler alone on a changing table. Even newborn infants turn and squirm when they are being changed.

6 Place the infant or toddler on his or her back. Take off the dirty diaper by lifting the infant's or toddler's legs and hips high enough to slide the dirty diaper away. Fold the diaper so that the mess is on the inside. Set the dirty diaper out of the way where the infant or toddler can't reach it. Lift up the infant or toddler, and clean with wipes or a washcloth.

Always clean from the front to the back, and be sure to separate the folds of the skin to remove all mess. Be gentle. When changing a boy, keep him covered with a wipe or a diaper as much as possible to avoid being sprayed.

7 Use one hand to hold the infant's or toddler's feet and lift up the bottom. Use the other hand to slip the open clean diaper under the infant's or toddler's bottom. Put the clean diaper under the infant or toddler with the folded part in front for a boy and in back for a girl.

8 Pull the diaper up between the infant's or toddler's legs. Overlap the back of the diaper on top of the front at the infant's or toddler's hips. Hold your fingers between the diaper and the infant or toddler, and pin on the outside of the diaper. The diaper should fit snugly but not bind. Put the rubber pants on over the diaper.

9 Dispose of the feces in the toilet, and then put the dirty diaper into the diaper pail. Make sure the changing surface is clean. After properly disposing of the dirty wipes, remove your gloves, and put them in the plastic trash bag. (See p. 58 for how to remove gloves.) Keep one hand on the infant or toddler at all times.

10 Wash the infant's or toddler's hands, and place him or her in a safe location while you wash your own hands.

● ●

Tearless Toileting Tips

◆ Some older toddlers and most preschoolers are learning to use the toilet. Follow the parents' or guardians' routine and ask what words or signals children use to tell they "have to go to the bathroom. (See the Family Interview Form, pp. 5–7.)

◆ Wash your hands before and after helping the child use the toilet. Be sure children wash their hands after toileting too.

◆ Some families have a child's potty. Some children sit on a full-sized toilet.

◆ Children who are already toilet trained sometimes still need help. They may need help unfastening their clothes, wiping themselves, or washing their hands. Girls need to wipe from front to back.

◆ Never make a big deal out of an accident because this might embarrass the child. Clean the child, and say it was a good try. Be sure to wear disposable gloves when cleaning the child.

◆ Encourage children to use the toilet frequently. Give children an opportunity to use the toilet before and after eating, before and after bed, and before and after activities such as playing outside. If children are showing signs that they need to use the bathroom, such as clutching at their pants, shivering, or jumping around, take them to the bathroom immediately.

Dogs have it easy with housebreaking!

DRESSING CHILDREN

◆ Ask the parents or guardians about dressing their children. (See Family Interview Form, pp. 5–7.)

◆ Give yourself enough time to change the child. Rushing makes the job more difficult and can upset the child.

◆ Let toddlers help with dressing by encouraging them to pull off their socks or pull a loose shirt over their heads. Let them help you undo snaps or buttons.

Dressing Safety

◆ Don't let children walk around in socks without slip-proof bottoms.

◆ To help prevent children from tripping, do not dress them in pants that are too long—or roll up the pant legs. Make sure shoes fit securely.

◆ Avoid dressing children in clothes that fasten with drawstrings, especially around the neck. A child can be strangulated by a hooded sweatshirt with a drawstring tie that catches on something.

UNDRESSING CHILDREN

1

Undo the snaps on the front of the shirt.

2

If the child is wearing a T-shirt or pullover shirt, first stretch the neck of the shirt and ease it over the child's head, gently past one ear, then the other. Gently slide the arm out of the sleeve on one side and then the other.

3

When undressing an infant, be sure to keep him or her safe and comfortable. Never leave the infant alone on the changing table.

DRESSING SKILL

1

To put on a clean shirt with snaps, open all snaps. Roll or scrunch up the sleeves. Reach through one sleeve, grasp the child's hand, and draw the hand and arm gently through the sleeve. Bring the shirt around the back of the child. Do the same with the other arm. Fasten the shirt.

2

To put on a T-shirt or pullover shirt, stretch the neck of the shirt so that it is larger than the child's head. Pull the neck opening over the head, keeping it away from the child's ears and face.

Reach through the sleeve opening, and gently draw one arm through it. Repeat on the other side. Always be careful to protect the child's eyes, ears, nose, and jaw.

3

Put the dirty laundry where the parents or guardians told you to put it. (See the Family Interview Form, pp. 5–7.)

REST AND SLEEP
● ● ●

- ◆ Ask the parents or guardians about the child's nap, rest, and bedtime routines. (See the Family Interview Form, pp. 5–7.)

- ◆ Help prepare the child for sleep by choosing quiet activities. Quiet activities include reading comforting stories and listening to soft music.

- ◆ Some children wake up or come out of quiet time in a calm way. Other children wake up noisy and ready to play.

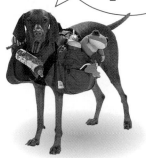

Quiet time is my favorite time... I could use a nap now!

● ●

Putting Children to Bed

1 About 15 minutes ahead of time, tell the child that bedtime or naptime is coming.

2 Check the infant's crib to remove toys, pillows, or any other soft, fluffy object that could choke or suffocate the infant. (See the Safety Inspection Checklist, pp. 45–46, for more bedtime safety tips.)

3 Put infants under 1 year of age to sleep on their backs face up. It is not safe for infants to sleep face down.

4 Massaging or rubbing the child's back can be a comforting way to help the child get to sleep.

5 Tell the child to sleep well, and say good night.

6 Check on the children every half hour. Make sure you stay where you are able to hear the children if they awaken.

7 Return children to bed if they get up. Comfort them if they have fears or nightmares. Be kind but firm in helping children.

BASIC CARE
● ● ●

"Factoid" Challenge

You are the navigator. Your mission is to search through the following statements to identify the "factoids" (true statements) from the decoys (false statements). Circle the "factoids," and cross out the decoys. Refer to these "factoids" for smooth basic care "flying."

1 **Wait until you begin basic care to find out what supplies you need.**

2 **All children like to be held and cuddled.**

3 **Let a child sleep with a light on if he or she wants.**

4 **Put an infant face down to sleep.**

5 **Let children eat with their hands if they want.**

6 **When children wet their pants or the bed, make a big deal out of it so they will remember never to do it again.**

7 **All families give basic care to their children in the same way.**

"Factoids": 3, 5, 9, 10, 11, 12

8 Play an active game and run outdoors with the children just before their bedtime so they'll be tired and want to go to bed.

9 It is normal for children to begin toilet training as early as 2 years and to complete toilet training as old as 5 years.

10 A clean floor is a safe place to change children's diapers and to put on their clothes.

11 Ask children frequently and regularly if they need to use the bathroom.

12 Wash the children's hands after changing their diapers.

13 Feed the children yourself because letting them feed themselves takes too long and makes a big mess.

CHECK-CALL-CARE
• • •

What Is an Emergency?

An emergency is a problem situation where action is needed right away because someone is injured or ill. The most important thing to do in any emergency is to stay calm.

Babysitters must know what to do in an emergency. If an infant or child is injured or sick or starts choking, you have to act fast.

How Do You Know It's an Emergency?

A babysitter needs to use his or her senses of sight, smell, touch, and hearing to determine whether there is an emergency. For example, you may see something unusual or hear an accident happen or someone call for help. You may even smell something that signals a problem, like smoke from a fire.

Life-Threatening Emergencies

In a life-threatening emergency, the child or infant needs medical care right away. These emergencies are life-threatening:

◆ The infant or child is unconscious.

◆ The infant or child is not breathing or is having trouble breathing.

◆ The infant or child has no heartbeat (or pulse).

◆ The infant or child has severe bleeding you cannot stop.

◆ The infant or child cannot move his or her arms or legs.

For any of these life-threatening emergencies, call 9-1-1 or the local emergency number. If someone is with you, have him or her call while you provide care. If you are alone in a life-threatening emergency, provide 1 minute of care before calling 9-1-1 or the local emergency number for help.

What to Do in an Emergency

For any emergency, always use the action steps Check-Call-Care. The order of Check-Call-Care may vary slightly based on the emergency situation and who is available to help.

Check the scene first.
◆ Look for any clues that show what happened. You might see something that looks like poison, for example, or something that caused an injury. Also make sure there is nothing that could hurt you or cause further injury to the infant or child.

Check the infant or child.
◆ See what is wrong. Tap the infant or child and shout to see if he or she is awake and breathing. Check for life-threatening emergencies first.

CALL

◆ Call 9-1-1 or the local emergency number. If someone is with you, have him or her call while you provide care. If you are alone in a life-threatening emergency, provide 1 minute of care before calling 9-1-1 or the local emergency number for help.

◆ If it is not an emergency, you might not have to call for medical help. For some minor problems, you can give first aid by yourself. For example, you can care for a minor cut or **scrape**.

CARE

◆ The care you give depends on the kind of emergency or problem.

◆ Use the First Aid Action Plans, which begin on p. 107 of this Babysitter's Handbook, as a guide to help you take care of the different kinds of injuries and illnesses infants or children may experience.

How to Call for Help

In an emergency, an infant or child may need medical help.
Call 9-1-1 or the local emergency number.

Is 9-1-1 used in your area? _____

If not, write your local emergency phone number here:

_____

Write your Poison Control Center (PCC) phone number here:

_____

Here's how to call:

1 Call 9-1-1 or the local emergency number.

2 Tell the dispatcher who answers the phone that you have an emergency.

3 Answer the questions the dispatcher asks, such as who you are, what happened, where the emergency is, the number you are calling from, how many people are injured, and what type of care, if any, is being given.

4 Don't hang up! Wait until the dispatcher tells you to hang up. He or she may need more information. The dispatcher also might tell you what to do. Follow his or her instructions.

The dispatcher will send medical help to your location to give care. An ambulance may arrive first, or police or firefighters may come to help if they can get there first.

First Aid Kit

Your first aid kit should have items you will need for an emergency. You can make your own or buy one. Make sure your first aid kit has the supplies you need and is ready to use before you go on the job. Always take your first aid kit with you when you babysit. If you take the children away from their home, such as to the park or for a walk, take the kit with you.

Keep the first aid kit away from the children. Some things in the kit can be dangerous for children. If you do not own a first aid kit, ask about the location in the home of the family's first aid kit when you are interviewing the parents or guardians. Ask to see the kit, and check it out to make sure it has the supplies you might need.

The *American Red Cross Safety and First Aid Kit* is available from your local American Red Cross. The Kit has the following supplies in it:

◆ Disposable gloves (two pairs)

◆ Hand wipes or towelettes (for when you do not have water available)

◆ Adhesive bandages in different sizes and shapes (kids like the ones in colors or with pictures on them)

◆ Gauze pads

◆ Roller gauze bandage

◆ Emergency Numbers and Family Information notepad

◆ Small flashlight

You may want to add the following items to your first aid kit, depending on your needs:

◆ Adhesive tape in different sizes

◆ Scissors

◆ Pen or pencil

◆ Tweezers

◆ Face mask or face shield for rescue breathing

◆ Zipper-lock bags

◆ Cold pack

◆ Batteries for the flashlight

◆ Anything else needed for the children you are babysitting

FiRST AiD
FOR BREATHING EMERGENCIES
● ● ●

What Is a Breathing Emergency?

A breathing emergency is when someone is not breathing or is having trouble breathing. If an infant or child has a breathing emergency, you need to act fast because the heart will stop soon if the infant or child is not getting air. First aid for a breathing emergency can save the infant's or child's life.

Breathing emergencies can occur for different reasons:

◆ An infant or child may be choking on an object, such as a piece of food or a small ball.

◆ An infant or child may have an **asthma** attack and not be able to breathe well.

◆ An infant or child may have an **allergic reaction** to a bee sting, and a swollen throat makes breathing difficult.

◆ An electric shock or drowning can cause breathing to stop.

Signals of a Breathing Emergency

The signals of a breathing emergency include—

◆ The infant or child may be agitated, dizzy, excited, or drowsy.

◆ The skin may be **pale, blue,** or **ashen.**

◆ The lips or fingernail beds may be blue.

◆ Breathing may be fast or slow.

◆ Breathing may be noisy, with the infant or child making sounds, such as **wheezing,** rasping, gurgling, or **crowing.**

◆ The infant or child may be grasping at his or her throat.

Check to Find Out What the Problem Is

In Lesson 6, you learned how to use the action steps Check-Call-Care in an emergency. When an infant or child is having trouble breathing, check him or her quickly to find out—

◆ If he or she can breathe. (Watch to see if the chest rises and falls.)

◆ If he or she can cough. (If he or she is coughing, don't stop him or her; tell the child to keep coughing.)

◆ If he or she can talk or cry. (Ask, "Can you breathe?")

If the child is coughing or can talk or cry, he or she is breathing—but still may be having trouble breathing. To help an infant or child with trouble breathing, see the First Aid Action Plans for Choking, pp. 118–122, and for Rescue Breathing, pp. 134–136.

First Aid for Someone Who Has Stopped Breathing

If an infant or child has stopped breathing, the first aid you give is called "rescue breathing." This is a method of blowing air into the child's mouth, or the infant's mouth and nose, to get air into the lungs. This method is described in the First Aid Action Plans for Rescue Breathing for an Infant, pp. 135–136, and for a Child, pp. 134–135. This care may be needed to save a life.

Face Shields and Masks

You may feel uncomfortable putting your mouth on someone else's to do rescue breathing, especially if it is someone you don't know. It's normal to worry about this. But you should know that the chance of getting a disease from rescue breathing is very low. Using special devices can lower that risk even more. They help protect you from blood and other body fluids.

You can use a simple face shield that is small enough to fit in your pocket or first aid kit. You just place this shield over the child's mouth and breathe through its opening. Some shields have mouthpieces that fit into the child's mouth. You press your mouth over the opening and breathe for the child. Other devices include masks with valves.

If you choose to use a face mask or shield, keep one with your first aid kit, or ask if the family has one. You can buy face masks or shields at some drugstores or medical supply stores and at your local American Red Cross.

Choking

Choking is a special kind of breathing problem that is common in children. A choking infant or child can quickly stop breathing, become unconscious, and die. That's why it is important to recognize when an infant or child is choking.

Signals of Choking

An infant or child may be choking if he or she is—

◆ Coughing hard but can't get the object unstuck from the airway.

◆ Coughing weakly or making a high-pitched sound while breathing.

◆ Unable to speak, cry, cough, or breathe.

◆ Clutching or grabbing at the throat.

◆ Unconscious.

For a choking infant or child, the first step is to get the object out and the air in. The care differs for an infant and a child because of the difference in body sizes. The care also differs depending on whether the infant or child is **conscious** or unconscious. Turn to the First Aid Action Plans for Choking:

◆ Choking, Conscious Child, pp. 118–119

◆ Choking, Conscious Infant, pp. 119–120

◆ Choking, Unconscious Child, pp. 120–121

◆ Choking, Unconscious Infant, pp. 121–122

FiRST AiD
FOR BLEEDING
EMERGENCIES
● ● ●

Bleeding is caused by a wound or injury. Infants and children get scrapes and scratches frequently. Blood vessels under the skin are like little pipes carrying blood throughout the body. If a blood vessel is torn or damaged, blood is lost.

Bleeding usually stops by itself in a few minutes, but sometimes it does not. The First Aid Action Plan for Bleeding, pp. 113–114, tells you how to care for a child who is bleeding.

Types of Bleeding

Bleeding that stops by itself in a few minutes is called minor bleeding. With a more serious wound or injury, like a deep cut, severe bleeding may occur. Blood can even squirt from a wound if a larger blood vessel deeper under the skin is damaged. In this case, first aid is needed immediately to stop the bleeding.

Types of Wounds

The first aid you give depends on the type of wound.

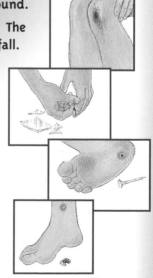

◆ Scrapes are the most common type of wound. The skin is rubbed or scraped away, often from a fall.

◆ Cuts can be caused by sharp objects, such as scissors, knives, or broken glass.

◆ Puncture wounds happen when a pointed object, like a nail, a piece of glass, or a knife, pierces deep through the skin. Bleeding can be severe, and there may be damage deeper in the body. Sometimes, however, puncture wounds bleed just a little or not at all.

◆ Bites and stings may occur from animals, insects, or humans. They can be minor or severe. (See the First Aid Action Plans for Bites and Stings, pp. 110–113.)

DECISION MAKING IN EMERGENCIES

• • •

Story Card 1

Your instructor will tell you how to fill out this page during class. Pretend that you are Alex.

1 Is it safe?

2 Check the scene. What happened? How can you tell?

3 Are the other children safe? How do you know? If they are not, what should you do?

4 Check the infant or child. Is he or she conscious or unconscious? How do you know?

5 Is the infant or child breathing? How do you know?

6 Does the infant or child have a pulse? How do you know?

7 Is the infant or child bleeding severely? How do you know?

8 Should you call anyone about this emergency?

Who?

Why?

When?

9 What should you do after making the call?

10 How could this situation have been prevented?

DECISION MAKING IN EMERGENCIES
• • •

Story Card 2

Your instructor will tell you how to fill out this page during class. Pretend that you are Moesha.

1 Is it safe?

2 Check the scene. What happened? How can you tell?

3 Are the other children safe? How do you know? If they are not, what should you do?

4 Check the infant or child. Is he or she conscious or unconscious? How do you know?

5 Is the infant or child breathing? How do you know?

6 Does the infant or child have a pulse? How do you know?

7 Is the infant or child bleeding severely? How do you know?

8 Should you call anyone about this emergency?

Who?

Why?

When?

9 What should you do after making the call?

10 How could this situation have been prevented?

DECISION MAKING IN EMERGENCIES
● ● ●

Story Card 3

Your instructor will tell you how to fill out this page during class. Pretend that you are Brad.

1 Is it safe?

2 Check the scene. What happened? How can you tell?

3 Are the other children safe? How do you know? If they are not, what should you do?

4 Check the infant or child. Is he or she conscious or unconscious? How do you know?

5 Is the infant or child breathing? How do you know?

6 Does the infant or child have a pulse? How do you know?

7 Is the infant or child bleeding severely? How do you know?

8 Should you call anyone about this emergency?

   Who?

   Why?

   When?

9 What should you do after making the call?

10 How could this situation have been prevented?

DECISION MAKING IN EMERGENCIES
• • •
Story Card 4

Your instructor will tell you how to fill out this page during class. Pretend that you are Amanda.

I Is it safe?

2 Check the scene. What happened? How can you tell?

3 Are the other children safe? How do you know? If they are not, what should you do?

4 Check the infant or child. Is he or she conscious or unconscious? How do you know?

5 Is the infant or child breathing? How do you know?

6 Does the infant or child have a pulse? How do you know?

7 Is the infant or child bleeding severely? How do you know?

8 Should you call anyone about this emergency?

Who?

Why?

When?

9 What should you do after making the call?

10 How could this situation have been prevented?

FIRST AID PUZZLE • • •

Complete the crossword puzzle, using the words missing in these first aid sentences.

a. Most important in any _ _ _ _ _ _ _ _ _: Stay calm.

b. Scrapes and a _ _ _ are examples of types of wounds.

c. An emergency is a problem situation where _ _ _ _ _ _ is needed right away because someone is injured or ill.

d. To call for help in an emergency, call 9-1-1 or your _ _ _ _ _ emergency phone number.

e. Keep your first aid kit away from _ _ _ _ _ _ _ _.

f. If an infant or child has _ _ _ _ _ _ _ breathing, the first aid you give is called "rescue breathing."

g. An infant or child may be choking if he or she is unable to speak, cry, _ _ _ _ _, or breathe.

h. _ _ _ _ _ _ bleeding is a signal of a life-threatening emergency.

Use the list below to help you select the correct words to complete the puzzle.

Bites	Minor	Local
Severe	Poison	Cut
Infants	Cough	Choking
Safety	Wheezing	Action
Emergency	Children	Stopped

Look at the answer key on the next page if you tried but still need help.

Use your first aid knowledge to solve this puzzle quicker than I can wag my tail!

Answers:

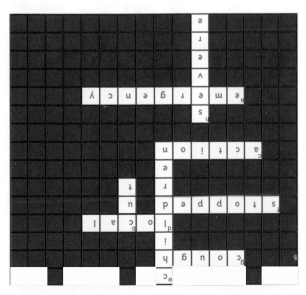

THE BUSINESS OF BABYSITTING

Getting Off to the Right Start in Babysitting

Not every babysitting job will be right for you. Knowing what you can do and what you like to do, as well as your limitations, will help you find the right jobs. You should also rate how well you did after each babysitting job is over. Doing these things will help you have a safe, responsible, and successful babysitting experience. They show that you take the responsibility of babysitting seriously—that you are a professional. You will also become a better babysitter over time.

Reporting to Your Parents or Guardians

◆ Discuss with your parents or guardians their overall expectations for you as a babysitter.

◆ Discuss each job with your parents or guardians before accepting the work.

◆ Remind them about the job before you go. Tell them when the job starts, how you will get to and from the job safely, and when you'll be back home.

◆ Discuss with them afterward anything unusual or disturbing that happened.

Professional Behavior from Beginning to End

What does it mean to be professional? Babysitting is a job that requires a lot of responsibility. People who hire you are trusting you with the care of their children and their house. They are looking for a lot of things when they hire a babysitter.

First, they want someone who is mature enough and has the right skills to watch their children safely. They also want someone who is reliable. It doesn't matter if you are the best babysitter in the world—if you are late or cancel appointments all the time, you won't continue to get job offers. Parents or guardians also want someone who gets along with their children. Being professional means all this. Having a professional attitude will get you more babysitting jobs.

Good Business Practices

Good business practices are guidelines for the ways you should act while on the job. As a professional babysitter, you should—

◆ Discuss with your parents or guardians where and when you are asked to babysit before you accept the job. Also let them know how many children you will be caring for, their ages, and any special conditions about the job (for example, you will be preparing a simple meal; you will be taking the children on an outing to the playground, park, or zoo; or you will be working with a child who has special needs).

◆ Make sure you are free to do the job and your family doesn't have anything scheduled.

◆ Dress for the job in clean, comfortable clothes.

◆ Get to the job early or on time.

◆ Learn the house rules where you are babysitting *before* the job starts. (See the Family Interview Form, pp. 5–7.)

◆ Treat the children and family with the same courtesy you expect for yourself.

◆ Report to the parents or guardians before you leave the job. (See the Babysitter's Report Record, pp. 22–23.)

◆ Never talk about what you see or hear in the homes where you babysit (except with your parents, guardians, or someone you trust).

◆ Discuss babysitting problems or concerns with someone you trust.

◆ Never look through belongings or rooms where you babysit unless the children's parents or guardians ask you to.

◆ Never cancel a babysitting job unless you have an emergency or are ill.

◆ Tell the parents or guardians as soon as you know you cannot babysit.

◆ Work to improve your babysitting skills.

Interviewing the Parents or Guardians and Assessing the Job

Not all babysitting jobs are the same. Some are harder than others. Find out as much as you can about the job during your interview with the parents or guardians. (See the Family Interview Form, pp. 5–7.) Ask about—

☐ *Transportation*. How are you going to get there and home safely?

☐ *Number of children*. Care for only as many children as you are sure you can handle safely. For most babysitters, that means no more than three children. For more than three children, you will need help. Ask if you can bring along a friend to help; your friend also should be paid.

☐ *Ages of children*. Younger children usually need more care. Infants need a lot of watching. Toddlers are always on the go. Preschoolers and school-aged children need your full attention too. Do not take jobs where you are expected to watch several young children by yourself.

☐ *Length of time*. Long hours make the job harder. While you are new to babysitting, limit your jobs to 2 or 3 hours.

☐ *Time of day*. Watching children at night while they sleep is usually easier than watching them during the day.

☐ *Responsibilities*. Do not say you will do other chores like cooking or bathing a child unless you have been trained to do so. Your first responsibility is to keep the children safe.

☐ *Children with special needs.* You might be a babysitter for a child with special emotional, physical, or learning needs or a child who is hard to control. Some children need special equipment like a wheelchair. Agree to babysit for children with special needs only if the parents or guardians train you in the special things you will need to do.

☐ *House rules.* Know the house rules for both yourself and the children.

Telephone Safety Tips

Always—

◆ Ask the parents or guardians how they want their phone answered.

◆ Write down the message, as well as the caller's name, the time of the call, and the caller's phone number.

◆ Use the phone for calls related to the job only, not for personal calls.

◆ Be polite.

◆ Call the parents or guardians, an adult you trust, or the police if you get a call that scares you.

◆ Make sure emergency phone numbers are posted by all phones.

◆ Make sure the address of where you are babysitting is posted by all phones.

EMERGENCY NUMBERS

POLICE 555-7777

FIRE 555-7777

Never—

◆ Tell callers that you are the babysitter or that the parents or guardians are away. Instead, say, "Mr. Rodriguez is busy right now. May I take a message?"

◆ Call your friends or have them call you while you're on the job. You could miss an important call from the children's parents or guardians, or you may not hear the children if they call to you or become ill.

Personal Safety Tips

Your own health and safety are just as important as the health and safety of the children you babysit.

◆ Know the parents or guardians and the families of the children you will babysit.

◆ Tell your parents or guardians where you will be, when to expect you home, and how to contact you. Know where they will be and how to contact them.

◆ If babysitting for a family makes you feel uncomfortable, don't babysit for them.

◆ Make your own arrangements to get to and from the job safely. Have a backup plan ready. (Example: If you are uncomfortable riding home with an employer, have a code word that you can use on the telephone to let your parents or guardians know that you need a ride home.)

◆ Do not wear jewelry that dangles or has sharp edges. It can scratch or hurt you or the children.

◆ Keep your clothing neat and your hair out of the way so they do not get caught in furniture or elsewhere.

◆ Keep your fingernails short and your hands clean to prevent the spread of germs.

◆ Do not babysit when you are sick.

◆ Do not use alcohol, drugs, or tobacco.

◆ Keep your first aid kit handy but out of the children's reach.

◆ Take your Babysitter's Handbook with you to the home. Use it as a reference while you're on the job.

◆ Know and respect your own limits. Don't take a job or try to do something you're not sure about.

I always have my Babysitter's Handbook when I Babysit!

Tips for Preventing Emergencies

In the Home

◆ Never open the door to strangers.

◆ Never open the door to delivery people. Tell them to leave the package at the door, or say that they have to come back another time.

◆ Never open the door to anyone, including the parents or guardians, before checking to see who is there. Look out through a peephole or window first.

◆ Never let anyone inside who is using alcohol or drugs, even if you know them.

◆ Never have your friends over to visit while you are babysitting.

◆ Never stay anywhere that you or the children are being threatened by a parent, guardian, or anyone else. Take the children immediately to a safe place. A safe place could be a neighbor's home; a school; a church, mosque, or synagogue; a local business; or a police or fire station.

◆ Never stay anywhere that you smell smoke or hear a fire or smoke alarm. Get the children and yourself outside. Ask a neighbor to call the fire department.

Outside the Home

◆ Never talk with strangers. If someone keeps trying to talk to you, take the children to a safe area.

◆ Never go outside to check out an unusual noise. If you are worried about it, call the parents or guardians, an adult you trust, or the police.

Special Concerns

Child abuse is the term for someone hurting a child physically, emotionally, or sexually. Some children who are abused are not fed, washed, or clothed properly.

◆ An abused child may have bruises, burns, or scars. Often, physically abused children are afraid of contact, such as hugging or being held.

◆ An abused child may have low self-esteem, seem very sad or cry a lot, act quiet, or be very loud and aggressive.

◆ A sexually abused child may know a lot about sex and may be afraid to undress or have physical contact with anyone. He or she may have signs of physical abuse.

If you think a child in your care has been abused, don't ask the child about it. Tell an adult you trust, like your parent or guardian or a teacher, about your concerns, and ask him or her what to do.

BABYSITTER'S SELF-ASSESSMENT TOOL

● ● ●

Answer these questions to discover your skills, abilities, likes, and dislikes regarding baby-sitting. There are no right or wrong answers. Update the Babysitter's Self-Assessment Tool every 6 months.

Background and Experience

1 The number of babysitting jobs I have had is—

___ None.   ___ 1–3.   ___ 4–6.   ___ 7–10.   ___ More than 10.

2 The most children I have cared for at one time is—

___ 1.   ___ 2.   ___ 3.   ___ 4.   ___ 5 or more.

3 The youngest child I have ever cared for is a(n)—

___ Infant (newborn to 12 months). ___ Preschooler (3 to 5 years).

___ Toddler (1 to 3 years). ___ School-aged child (5 to 8 years).

4 The oldest child I have ever cared for is a(n)—

___ Infant (newborn to 12 months). ___ Preschooler (3 to 5 years).

___ Toddler (1 to 3 years).   ___ School-aged child
                                      (5 to 8 years).

5 The longest babysitting job I ever had lasted—

___ 1 hour.   ___ 2–3 hours.   ___ 3–5 hours.   ___ 5–8 hours.

___ More than 8 hours.

6 I have accepted babysitting jobs— (check all that apply)

___ On weekdays.   ___ In my neighborhood.

___ On weeknights.   ___ Outside my neighborhood.

___ On weekend days.

___ On weekend nights.

Special Skills and Abilities

7 My special abilities that make me a great babysitter are— (check all that apply)

___ Music.

___ Arts and crafts.

___ Sports.

___ Good student.

___ Storytelling.

___ Patience.

___ Creativity.

___ Problem solving.

___ Calmness in an emergency.

___ Other: _____.

8 My leadership skills include— (check all that apply)

___ Using the FIND Decision-Making Model to make decisions.

___ Communicating well with children.

___ Recognizing and respecting differences among children and families.

___ Correcting misbehavior appropriately.

___ Recognizing the developmental stages of children at different ages.

9 My safety skills include— (check all that apply)

___ Getting information before the job begins.

___ Recognizing and removing or limiting safety-related problems.

___ Supervising children at all times.

___ Choosing appropriate play for children at different ages.

___ Keeping my *American Red Cross Safety and First Aid Kit* out of the children's reach.

___ Being a role model for safety.

___ Using the Safety Inspection Checklist, pp. 45–46.

10 My basic care skills include— (check all that apply)

____ Following the family's instructions.

____ Washing my hands and helping children wash their hands.

____ Diapering children and helping them use the toilet.

____ Feeding children with a bottle or a spoon.

____ Helping children get rest and sleep.

____ Holding children correctly.

____ Giving appropriate care for children at different ages.

11 My first aid skills include— (check all that apply)

____ Recognizing and acting appropriately in an emergency.

____ Recognizing and giving the right care to a child who is ill or injured.

____ Giving appropriate care for children at different ages.

Preferences

12 I prefer to care for— (check all that apply)

____ One child at a time.

____ Several children at a time.

____ Infants.

____ Toddlers.

____ Preschoolers.

____ School-aged children.

13 The time of day I prefer to babysit is—

____ Weekdays.   ____ Weeknights.

____ Weekend days.   ____ Weekend nights.

14 I prefer to get rides to and from jobs—

____ From my parents.   ____ From the children's parents or guardians.

____ On my own.

15 I absolutely do NOT want to babysit when _____

_____.

Parent Assessment

Instructions:
Ask your parents or guardians these questions. Be sure they approve and support your babysitting plans.

16 My parents or guardians will— (check all that apply)

____ Take me to and from jobs.

____ Be available by phone when I am on the job.

____ Tell me which jobs they will not allow me to accept.

____ Tell me their rules for my babysitting jobs.

____ Work with me to make sure that my *American Red Cross Safety and First Aid Kit* is fully supplied for each babysitting job.

17 My parents or guardians will not allow me to accept these jobs:

18 My parents' or guardians' rules for my babysitting jobs are—

BLANK RESUME

● ● ●

Use the blank resume on the next page to help you get babysitting jobs. Fill in the blanks to make your personal resume. Then you can print or type your resume on a clean sheet of paper to give to parents who may want to hire you. Use the space below to draw what you would like your resume to look like.

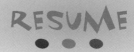

RESUME

Name: _____

Address: _____

Phone: _____

Education: Your school _____

Your grade _____

Training: **American Red Cross Babysitter's Training course**

With training in helping children behave, basic child care, safety and safe play, first aid, professionalism

Additional Training: [Include whatever applies]

Babysitting Experience:

Hobbies:

Skills and abilities from my Babysitter's Self-Assessment Tool:

References: **[List here the names and phone numbers of people you babysat for in the past year who say it is okay to use them as references.]**

Self-Evaluation after the Job

Things I need to think about after I finish a babysitting job:

◆ How well did I do on this job?

◆ What went well?

◆ What happened that I was afraid I couldn't handle?

◆ What should I do differently next time?

◆ Could I have better prepared myself for this job? How?

◆ Will I babysit for this family again? If not, why not?

◆ Other comments:

SHINING STAR GAME

● ● ●

Instructions:
Unscramble the words on leadership and professionalism to fill up the briefcase. Use the sample scramble to help you get started.

Sample

Before accepting a babysitting job, use the [ymafli tinwvieer] Form to learn as much as you can from the parents or guardians about their children and their house rules. (Answer: Family Interview)

I You are a leader because children look to you as the [nispslere-bo] person in charge.

_____

2 A good leader and role model [muntccaiesom] well with both the children and their parents or guardians.

_____

3 Part of having a [ssfproealion] attitude is being reliable.

_____

4 Good [sseusbin cctiespar] are guidelines for the ways you should act while on the job.

_____

5 Use the FIND model to help you with situations that require careful [iscedion gminka].

_____

FiRST AiD ACTiON PLANS

CONTENTS

Special Note: This course does not provide you with certification in first aid or CPR. It does, however, provide you with some knowledge and skill practice in these areas. If you want certification, it is recommended that you enroll in an American Red Cross CPR or First Aid course.

Emergency Action Steps

CHECK

CALL

CARE

Allergic Reactions

Notes

- Allergic reactions can be caused by certain foods, medications, bites or stings, or poisonous plants.
- They may cause swelling of the face, neck, and tongue.
- They may cause trouble breathing and make the chest and throat feel tight.
- They may cause rash, hives, or itching.
- The child may feel dizzy or confused.

First Aid Steps

CHECK the scene and the infant or child. Use disposable gloves when you might touch any body fluid.

CALL 9-1-1 if the infant or child shows any of the following signals:

- Trouble breathing
- Uncontrollable coughing or wheezing
- Tightness in the chest or throat
- Swelling of the face, neck, or tongue

CARE for the infant or child:

- Help the infant or child into a position that is comfortable for breathing.
- Provide the infant or child with his or her prescribed medication as directed by the parents or guardians.

◆ Call the parents or guardians if the infant or child has—

- Hives.
- Pale, gray, or flushed skin.
- An itchy rash that is spreading.
- Nausea or vomiting.
- Swelling anywhere other than the face, neck, or tongue (see above).

◆ Provide care until the ambulance personnel or the parents or guardians arrive and take over.

◆ Fill out the Babysitter's Report Record (pp. 22–23).

◆ Report to the parents or guardians when they arrive.
See also Vomiting, p. 140.

Bites, Animal and Human

Notes (Animal Bites)

- Get the infant or child away from the animal if you can do it safely.
- Report the bite to the local authorities (animal-control officer or other law enforcement officer) unless it is a family pet.
- Try to remember what the animal looked like and where you saw it last.

Note (Human Bites)

- A human bite can cause serious infection.

First Aid Steps

CHECK the scene and the infant or child. Use disposable gloves when you might touch any body fluid.

CALL 9-1-1 if the wound is large or deep or bleeds severely.

CARE for the infant or child:

Stop the bleeding (see Bleeding, p. 113–114).

If the wound is minor—

- Wash the bite area with soap and water.
- Cover the bite with a dressing and bandage.
- Help the infant or child rest comfortably.

◆ Call the parents or guardians and ask them to return home immediately.

◆ Provide care until the ambulance personnel or the parents or guardians arrive and take over.

◆ Fill out the Babysitter's Report Record (pp. 22–23).

◆ Report to the parents or guardians when they arrive.

See also Bleeding, pp. 113–114.

Bites, Snake

Note

- Do not try to catch the snake, but remember what it looked like, and tell this to the ambulance personnel.

First Aid Steps

CHECK the scene and the infant or child. Use disposable gloves when you might touch any body fluid.

CALL 9-1-1. Have someone else call if possible.

CARE for the infant or child:

- Wash the bite area with soap and water.

- Cover the area with a bandage.

- Keep the injured body part still and lower than the heart.

- Keep the infant or child calm and still.

◆ Call the parents or guardians and ask them to return home immediately.

◆ Provide care until the ambulance personnel or the parents or guardians arrive and take over.

◆ Fill out the Babysitter's Report Record (pp. 22–23).

◆ Report to the parents or guardians when they arrive.

Bites, Spider

Note

- Do not try to catch the spider, but remember what it looked like, and tell this to the ambulance personnel.

First Aid Steps

CHECK the scene and the infant or child. Use disposable gloves when you might touch any body fluid.

CALL 9-1-1 if the infant or child has a reaction to the bite that involves—

- Trouble breathing.

- Uncontrollable coughing or wheezing.

- Swelling of the face, neck, or tongue.

CARE for the infant or child:

- Wash the bite area with soap and water.

- Apply a cold pack, such as ice in a plastic bag, to the bite. Place a thin cloth or towel between the skin and the cold pack.

◆ Call the parents or guardians and ask them to return home immediately.

◆ Provide care until the ambulance personnel or the parents or guardians arrive and take over.

◆ Fill out the Babysitter's Report Record (pp. 22–23).

◆ Report to the parents or guardians when they arrive.

See also Allergic Reactions, p. 109.

Bites, Tick

First Aid Steps

CHECK the scene and the infant or child. Use disposable gloves when you might touch any body fluid.

CARE for the infant or child:

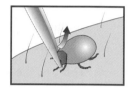

- Use tweezers to grasp the tick as close to the infant's or child's skin as possible. Pull the tick out slowly to avoid breaking or tearing the tick.

- Wash the bite area with soap.

◆ Fill out the Babysitter's Report Record (pp. 22–23). Note the location of the tick bite.

◆ Report to the parents or guardians when they arrive.

Bites and Stings, Insect

Notes

- Bites and stings may be life-threatening if the infant or child has an allergic reaction (see Allergic Reactions, p. 109).

- Watch for signals of an allergic reaction, and get help immediately if a reaction occurs.

- See also Bites, Tick above; Bites, Spider (p. 111–112).

First Aid Steps

CHECK the scene and the infant or child. Use disposable gloves when you might touch any body fluid.

CALL 9-1-1 if the child has an allergic reaction (see Allergic Reactions, p. 109).

CARE for the infant or child:

- Remove any stinger by scraping it away with a stiff object like a plastic card such as a credit card, a bank card, or an identification card.
- Wash the area of the bite or sting with soap and water.
- Cover the area to keep it clean.
- Apply a cold pack, such as ice in a plastic bag, to the bite or sting. Place a thin cloth between the skin and the cold pack.

◆ Call the parents or guardians if the infant or child—

- Looks or feels ill.
- Has an itchy rash that is spreading.
- Has nausea or vomiting.

◆ Provide care until the ambulance personnel or the parents or guardians arrive and take over.

◆ Fill out the Babysitter's Report Record (pp. 22–23).

◆ Report to the parents or guardians when they arrive.

See also Allergic Reactions, p. 109; Vomiting, p. 140.

Bleeding

Note

- Any serious bleeding can quickly become life-threatening.

First Aid Steps

CHECK the scene and the infant or child. Use disposable gloves when you might touch any body fluid.

CALL 9-1-1 if—

- Bleeding does not stop within a few minutes.
- Blood is spurting from the wound.
- The wound is on the stomach, the chest, or a joint, or there is a large wound to the hands or feet.
- You can see muscle or bone inside the wound.
- The wound is longer than 1 inch or is deep.
- The wound has an object stuck in it (see Wounds, with Object, p. 141).

- Skin or body parts have been partially or completely torn away.

CARE for the infant or child:

- Put a gauze pad or clean cloth over the wound, and apply pressure.

- Lift the wounded part above the level of the heart, unless you think there are broken bones.

- Cover the gauze pad with a roller bandage.

- If blood soaks through, put more gauze pads and another roller bandage on top of the first bandage. Do not remove the first gauze pad and bandage.

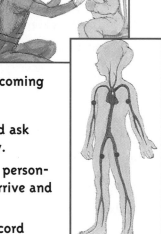

- If bleeding from arms or legs still does not stop, apply pressure at pressure points.

- Keep the infant or child from becoming chilled or too warm.

◆ Call the parents or guardians, and ask them to return home immediately.

◆ Provide care until the ambulance personnel or the parents or guardians arrive and take over.

◆ Fill out the Babysitter's Report Record (pp. 22–23).

Report to the parents or guardians when they arrive.

Burns

Notes

- Burns can be caused by heat, chemicals, electricity, and the sun.

- Never go near an injured infant or child who is touching an electrical wire until you are ABSOLUTELY sure the power is turned off.

First Aid Steps

CHECK the scene and the infant or child. Use disposable gloves when you might touch any body fluid.

CALL 9-1-1 for burns that—

- Involve trouble breathing.
- Cover more than one body part.
- Occur on the head, neck, hands, feet, or genitals.
- Result from chemicals, explosion, or electricity.
- Are deep (the skin has blisters or looks brown or black).

CARE for the infant or child:

- Remove the infant or child from the heat source.
- Cool the burn with water, unless it is an electrical burn (keep an electrical burn dry).
- Continuously flush chemical burns with cool water until the ambulance personnel arrive and take over. Remove any clothing that may trap chemicals against the skin.
- Cover the burn with clean, dry dressings.
- Loosely bandage the dressing in place to prevent infection and reduce pain, or cover the burned area with a dry sheet.
- Keep the infant or child from becoming chilled or too warm.
- Help the infant or child rest comfortably.

◆ Call the parents or guardians, and ask them to return home immediately.

◆ Provide care until the ambulance personnel or parents or guardians arrive and take over.

◆ Fill out the Babysitter's Report Record (pp. 22–23).

◆ Report to the parents or guardians when they arrive.

Checking a Conscious Infant or Child

First Aid Steps

CHECK the scene. Use disposable gloves when you might touch any body fluid.

CHECK the infant or child by—

Asking questions such as—

- What happened?

- Are you having any trouble breathing?

- Are you in pain?

- Where are you hurt?

- Or call out the infant's or child's name to check for a response.

Note: Do not ask the child to move any body areas that have discomfort or pain or if you suspect an injury to the head, neck, or back.

Check toe to head:

- Before you begin, tell the child what you are going to do, or talk in a soothing manner to an infant.

- Look over the body in general.

- Look carefully for bleeding, cuts, bruises, and obvious deformities.

Check the hips and legs:

- Check one leg at a time.

Ask the child to—

- Move the toes, foot, and ankle.

- Bend the leg.

Check the arms:

- Check one arm at a time.

Ask the child to—

- Move the hands and fingers.

- Bend the arm.

Check the chest and stomach:

- Ask the child to take a deep breath and blow air out.

- Ask the child if there is any pain with breathing.

Check the shoulders:

- Ask the child to shrug his or her shoulders.

Check the neck:

> *Note:* pain, discomfort, or inability to move.
>
> If the child is not in pain and you do not suspect an injury to the neck, ask the child to move his or her head slowly from side to side.

Check the head:

- Look at the scalp, face, ears, eyes, nose, and mouth for cuts, bumps, bruises, and depressions.

- Notice if the infant or child is drowsy, not alert, or confused.

Check skin appearance and temperature:

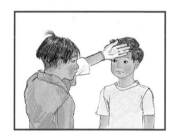

- Feel the infant's or child's forehead with the back of your hand.

- Look at the infant's or child's face and lips.

  Ask yourself, is the skin—

  - Cold or hot?

  - Unusually wet or dry?

  - Pale, bluish, ashen, or flushed?

  - Covered with hives or rash?

If the child can move all body parts without pain or discomfort and has no signals of life-threatening emergencies—

- Have him or her rest for a few minutes in a sitting position.

- Help the child slowly stand when he or she is ready.

CALL 9-1-1 if—

- A life-threatening problem, such as trouble breathing, becomes obvious.

- The infant or child cannot move a body part without pain.

CARE for any conditions you find.

◆ Call the parents or guardians, and explain the infant's or child's condition.

◆ Provide care until the ambulance personnel or the parents or guardians arrive and take over.

◆ Fill out the Babysitter's Report Record (pp. 22–23).

◆ Report to the parents or guardians when they arrive.

Choking, Conscious Child

Notes

● A child who cannot speak, cough, cry, or breathe may be choking.

● A child who can cough only weakly or is making high-pitched sounds may be choking.

First Aid Steps

CHECK the scene and the child. Use disposable gloves when you might touch any body fluid.

CALL 9-1-1. Have someone else call if possible.

CARE for the child:

● Stand or kneel behind the child, and put the thumb side of your fist just above the child's belly button. Grasp your fist with your other hand.

● Give quick, upward thrusts until the object is coughed up or the child can cough, speak, breathe, or cry—or becomes unconscious.

● If the child becomes unconscious, lower him or her gently to the floor. Call 9-1-1 if you have not already called. Go to the First Aid Action Plan for Choking, Unconscious Child, pp. 120–121.

● If the child can cough, speak, breathe, or cry, help him or her rest comfortably.

◆ Call the parents or guardians once the object is removed or the ambulance personnel arrive and take over, and ask them to return home immediately.

- Provide care until the ambulance personnel or the parents or guardians arrive and take over.
- Fill out the Babysitter's Report Record (pp. 22–23).
- Report to the parents or guardians when they arrive.

Choking, Conscious Infant

Notes

- An infant who cannot cough, cry, breathe, or make other sounds may be choking.
- An infant who can cough only weakly or is making high-pitched sounds, may be choking.

First Aid Steps

CHECK the scene and the infant. Use disposable gloves when you might touch any body fluid.

CALL 9-1-1. Have someone else call if possible.

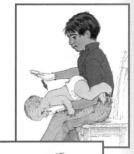

CARE for the infant:

- Hold the infant facedown on your arm. Rest your arm on your thigh, with the infant's head lower than the body.
- With the heel of your hand, give 5 back blows between the infant's shoulder blades.
- Support the infant, and turn him or her faceup on your other thigh.

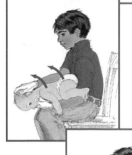

- Put 2 or 3 fingers on the center of the infant's breastbone, just below the nipples, and give 5 chest thrusts, about 1 inch deep.
- Continue 5 back blows and 5 chest thrusts until the infant can cough, breathe, or cry—or becomes unconscious.
- If the infant becomes unconscious, lower him or her gently to the floor. Call 9-1-1 if you have not already called. Go to the First Aid Action Plan for Choking, Unconscious Infant, pp. 121–122.
- If the infant can cough, breathe, or cry, help him or her rest comfortably.

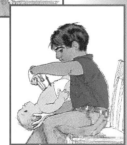

- ◆ Call the parents or guardians once the object is removed or the ambulance personnel arrive and take over, and ask them to return home immediately.
- ◆ Provide care until the ambulance personnel or the parents or guardians arrive and take over.
- ◆ Fill out the Babysitter's Report Record (pp. 22–23).
- ◆ Report to the parents or guardians when they arrive.

Choking, Unconscious Child

First Aid Steps

CHECK the scene and the child. Use disposable gloves when you might touch any body fluid.

CALL 9-1-1 after providing 1 minute of care if you are alone. Have someone else call if possible.

CARE for the child:

- Tap the child on the shoulder and shout to see if he or she responds.
- If there is no response, tilt the head back slightly while lifting the chin.
- Look, listen, and feel for breathing for about 5 seconds.
- If there is no breathing, give 2 slow breaths.
- If the breaths do not go in, retilt the head and try the breaths again.
- If the breaths still do not go in, place the heel of one hand just above the child's belly button. Put your other hand on top, and give 5 quick, upward thrusts.
- Grasp the lower jaw and tongue, and look in the mouth. If you see an object, sweep it out with your finger.
- Tilt the head back slightly while lifting the chin, and give 2 slow breaths.

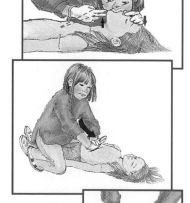

- If the breaths go in, the airway is open. Check the pulse to see if CPR is needed (see CPR, Child, pp. 123–125).
- If the breaths do not go in, retilt the head, and try 2 breaths again.
- If the breaths still do not go in, the airway is blocked. Repeat the thrusts, object check, head tilt, 2 slow breaths, head retilt, and 2 slow breaths until the breaths go in.

◆ Call the parents or guardians as soon as ambulance personnel arrive and take over.

◆ Provide care until the ambulance personnel or the parents or guardians arrive and take over.

◆ Fill out the Babysitter's Report Record (pp. 22–23).

Report to the parents or guardians when they arrive.

Choking, Unconscious Infant

First Aid Steps

CHECK the scene and the infant. Use disposable gloves when you might touch any body fluid.

CALL 9-1-1 after providing 1 minute of care if you are alone. Have someone else call if possible.

CARE for the infant:

- Tap the infant on the shoulder and shout to see if he or she responds.
- If there is no response, tilt the head back slightly while lifting the chin.
- Look, listen, and feel for breathing for about 5 seconds.
- If there is no breathing, cover the infant's nose and mouth with your mouth and give 2 slow breaths.
- If the breaths do not go in, retilt the head and try the breaths again.

- If the breaths still do not go in, hold the infant facedown on your arm. Rest your arm on your thigh, with the infant's head lower than the body.

- With the heel of your hand, give 5 back blows between the infant's shoulder blades.

- Support the infant, and turn him or her faceup on your other thigh.

- Put 2 or 3 fingers on the center of the infant's breastbone just below the nipples, and give 5 chest thrusts, about 1 inch deep.

- Place the infant on a safe, flat surface. Grasp the lower jaw and tongue, and look in the mouth. If you see an object, sweep it out with your finger.

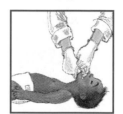

- Tilt the head back slightly while lifting the chin, and give 2 slow breaths.

- If the breaths go in, the airway is open. Check the pulse to see if CPR is needed (see CPR, Infant, pp. 125–126).

- If the breaths do not go in, retilt the head, and try 2 breaths again.

- If the breaths still do not go in, the airway is blocked. Repeat the back blows, chest thrusts, object check, head tilt, 2 slow breaths, head retilt, and 2 slow breaths until the breaths go in.

◆ Call the parents or guardians as soon as ambulance personnel arrive and take over.

◆ Provide care until the ambulance personnel or the parents or guardians arrive and take over.

◆ Fill out the Babysitter's Report Record (pp. 22–23).

◆ Report to the parents or guardians when they arrive.

Cold Emergencies

Notes
- Hypothermia and frostbite are cold emergencies.
- Frostbite is the freezing of body parts. The skin may look waxy, flushed, white, gray, or blue.
- Hypothermia is the general cooling of the body. The infant or child may be shivering or drowsy.

First Aid Steps

CHECK the scene and the infant or child. Use disposable gloves when you might touch any body fluid.

CALL 9-1-1 if the infant or child—

- Is unconscious.
- Is very drowsy or sleepy when he or she should not be.
- Has no feeling in a part of his or her body.

CARE for the infant or child:

- Gently move the infant or child to a warm place.
- Give rescue breathing if the infant or child is not breathing (see Rescue Breathing, Child, pp. 134–135; Rescue Breathing, Infant, pp. 135–136) or CPR if there is no heartbeat (see CPR, Child, pp. 123–125; CPR, Infant, pp. 125–126).
- Remove any wet clothing, and dry the infant or child.
- Warm the infant or child slowly by wrapping him or her in blankets or by putting on dry clothing. Hot water bottles and chemical hot packs may be used when first wrapped in a towel or blanket before placing on an infant or child.
- Do not rub frostbitten parts. Loosely bandage the affected area with dry dressings.

- ◆ Call the parents or guardians, and ask them to return home immediately.
- ◆ Provide care until the ambulance personnel or the parents or guardians arrive and take over.
- ◆ Fill out the Babysitter's Report Record (pp. 22–23).
- ◆ Report to the parents or guardians when they arrive.

CPR, Child

First Aid Steps

CHECK the scene and the child. Use disposable gloves when you might touch any body fluid.

CALL 9-1-1 after providing 1 minute of care if you are alone. Have someone else call if possible.

CARE for the child:

- Tap the child on the shoulder and shout to see if he or she responds.
- If there is no response, tilt the head back slightly while lifting the chin.
- Look, listen, and feel for breathing for about 5 seconds.

If the child is not breathing—

- Pinch the nose shut, and give 2 slow breaths.
- Check for a pulse at the side of the neck for about 5 to 10 seconds.

If there is no pulse and the child is not breathing—

- Keep the child's head tilted back with one hand.
- Place the heel of your other hand in the center of the chest directly over the breastbone.

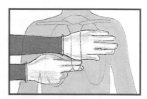

- Push down on the chest 5 times. Each compression should be about 1½ inches deep. Count "one, two, three, four, five."
- Give 1 slow breath.
- Call 9-1-1 if you have not already called.

- Repeat the sets of 5 compressions and 1 breath for about 1 minute.
- Recheck the pulse and breathing for about 5 seconds. If there is still no pulse, keep giving sets of 5 compressions and 1 breath until the ambulance personnel arrive and take over or the child has a pulse and is breathing.

- Recheck the pulse and breathing every few minutes.

◆ Call the parents or guardians as soon as the ambulance personnel arrive and take over.

- Provide care until the ambulance personnel or the parents or guardians arrive and take over.
- Fill out the Babysitter's Report Record (pp. 22–23).
- Report to the parents or guardians when they arrive.

CPR, Infant

First Aid Steps

CHECK the scene and the infant. Use disposable gloves when you might touch any body fluid.

CALL 9-1-1 after providing 1 minute of care if you are alone. Have someone else call if possible.

CARE for the infant:

- Tap the infant on the shoulder and shout to see if he or she responds.
- If there is no response, tilt the head back slightly while lifting the chin.
- Look, listen, and feel for breathing for about 5 seconds.

If the infant is not breathing—

- Cover the infant's nose and mouth with your mouth, and give 2 slow breaths.
- Check for a pulse on the inside of the upper arm for about 5 to 10 seconds.

If there is no pulse and the infant is not breathing—

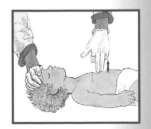

- Keep your hand on the infant's forehead.
- Put 2 or 3 fingers on the center of the infant's breastbone just below the nipples, and push down on the chest 5 times. Each compression should be about 1 inch deep. Count "one, two, three, four, five."
- Give 1 slow breath.
- Call 9-1-1 if you have not already called.
- Repeat the sets of 5 compressions and 1 breath for about 1 minute.

- Recheck the pulse and breathing for 5 seconds. If there is still no pulse, keep giving sets of 5 compressions and 1 breath until the ambulance personnel arrive and take over or the infant has a pulse and is breathing.

- Recheck the pulse and breathing every few minutes.

◆ Call the parents or guardians as soon as the ambulance personnel arrive and take over.

◆ Provide care until the ambulance personnel or the parents or guardians arrive and take over.

◆ Fill out the Babysitter's Report Record (pp. 22–23).

◆ Report to the parents or guardians when they arrive.

Ear Injury, Object in Ear

First Aid Steps

CHECK the scene and the infant or child. Use disposable gloves when you might touch any body fluid.

CALL 9-1-1 if the infant or child is bleeding or if fluid is draining from inside the ear.

CARE for the infant or child:

- Ask the child to turn his or her head to point the ear down. The object may fall out, or you may be able to gently pull the object from the ear with your fingers. Do not put any tools in the ear to try to remove the object.

- Pull down on the earlobe so that the object can fall out.

- If the child has an insect in the ear, have him or her turn the head to point the ear up. The insect may crawl out. It is frightening for a child to hear and feel an insect moving in the ear. Help the child remain calm.

- Cover the ear lightly with a sterile dressing.

- Help the infant or child rest comfortably.

◆ Call the parents or guardians if the object does not come out. Explain the infant's or child's condition, and ask them to return home immediately.

- ◆ Provide care until the ambulance personnel or the parents or guardians arrive and take over.
- ◆ Fill out the Babysitter's Report Record (pp. 22–23).
- ◆ Report to the parents or guardians when they arrive.

Eye Injury

Notes

- There may be injury around the eye and to the eyeball itself.
- Damage to the eyeball is very serious and can cause blindness.

First Aid Steps

CHECK the scene and the infant or child. Use disposable gloves when you might touch any body fluid.

CALL 9-1-1 immediately if there is an object sticking out from the eye.

If there is an object sticking out from the eye—

- Have the child rest on his or her back.
- Do not try to remove the object.
- Do not disturb an object in the eye. Hold the child's head still.

If there is a chemical in the eye, gently flush the eye with water, and go to the First Aid Action Plan for Burns, pp. 114–115.

CARE for the infant or child:

If there is a small object, such as dirt, in the eye—

- Have the child blink to try to flush the eye with tears.
- Gently flush the eye with cool water. Flush the eye from the nose outward. Use the spray hose on a kitchen sink or a cup of water.
- If the object will not come out, close the eyelid and loosely cover the eye with a gauze pad.
- Help the infant or child rest comfortably.

- ◆ Call the parents or guardians if the object does not come out. Explain the infant's or child's condition, and ask them to return immediately.
- ◆ Provide care until the ambulance personnel or the parents or guardians arrive and take over.

◆ Fill out the Babysitter's Report Record (pp. 22–23).

◆ Report to the parents or guardians when they arrive.

Head, Neck, and Back Injuries

Notes

- If there is an injury to the head, there may also be injuries to the neck or back.

- Always look for a head, neck, or back injury in these situations:
  - A hard object hit the top of the infant's or child's head.
  - The infant or child fell from a height greater than the infant's or child's height.
  - The infant or child was found unconscious for unknown reasons.
  - An injury penetrated the head or trunk.
  - There was an accident in which the child's helmet was cracked or broken.
  - There was an incident involving a lightning strike.

First Aid Steps

CHECK the scene and the infant or child. Use disposable gloves when you might touch any body fluid.

CALL 9-1-1. Have someone else call if possible.

CARE for the infant or child:

- Place your hands on both sides of the infant's or child's head to keep it from moving.
- Check for breathing.
- If the child is not breathing, begin rescue breathing (see Rescue Breathing, Child, pp. 134–135; Rescue Breathing, Infant, pp. 135–136) or CPR (see CPR, Child, pp. 123–125; CPR, Infant, pp. 125–126).
- Stop any bleeding (see Bleeding, pp 113–114).
- Prevent the infant or child from getting chilled or too warm.
- Keep the infant or child still and comfortable.

◆ Call the parents or guardians as soon as the ambulance personnel arrive and take over.

- Provide care until the ambulance personnel or the parents or guardians arrive and take over.
- Fill out the Babysitter's Report Record (pp. 22–23).
- Report to the parents or guardians when they arrive.

Heat Emergencies

Notes

- Heat emergencies are caused by overexposure to heat or being too active on a hot day.
- The child may feel weak and tired, have a headache, or feel dizzy.
- The skin may be hot, cool, moist, or dry, depending on the stage of the problem.

First Aid Steps

CHECK the scene and the infant or child. Use disposable gloves when you might touch any body fluid.

CALL 9-1-1 if the infant or child—

- Is dizzy or becomes unconscious.
- Begins to vomit.
- Refuses water.

CARE for the infant or child:

- Move the infant or child out of the heat immediately and to a cool place.
- Remove sweat-soaked clothing.
- Apply cool, wet cloths or a cold pack, such as ice in a plastic bag. Place a cloth or towel between the skin and the cold pack.
- Fan the infant or child.
- If the infant or child is conscious and not nauseated, give him or her cool water to drink.
- Help the infant or child rest comfortably.

- Call the parents or guardians, explain the infant's or child's condition, and ask them to return home immediately.
- Provide care until the ambulance personnel or the parents or guardians arrive and take over.

◆ Fill out the Babysitter's Report Record (pp. 22–23).

◆ Report to the parents or guardians when they arrive.

Mouth Injuries

Note

- The mouth may be injured on the inside or outside. The injury may affect the cheeks, tongue, lips, or teeth.

First Aid Steps

CHECK the scene and the infant or child. Use disposable gloves when you might touch any body fluid.

CALL 9-1-1 if the infant or child—

- Has signals of a head, neck, or back injury (see Head, Neck, and Back Injuries, pp. 128–129).
- Becomes unconscious.
- Has trouble breathing.
- Has bleeding that cannot be easily controlled.

CARE for the infant or child:

- If you don't suspect a serious head, neck, or back injury—

  Have the child lean slightly forward, or place the infant or child on his or her side to prevent swallowing blood, which may cause nausea or vomiting.

- For bleeding inside the cheek—

  Place a folded sterile dressing inside the mouth against the wound and apply pressure.

- For bleeding outside the cheek—

  Put pressure directly on the wound with a sterile dressing.

- If an object is embedded in the cheek, go to the First Aid Action Plan for Wounds, with Object, p. 141.

- For bleeding tongue or lips—

  Put direct pressure on the area with a sterile dressing.

  Apply a cold pack, such as ice in a plastic bag. Place a cloth or towel between the skin and the cold pack.

- If a tooth has been knocked out—

    Stop any bleeding by having the child bite down on a rolled sterile dressing put in the space left by the tooth.

    Save any teeth by placing them in a container of milk, if possible, or water.

    Check for head, neck, and back injuries (see Head, Neck, and Back Injuries, pp. 128–129).

◆ Call the parents or guardians and ask them to return home immediately. (The child needs to go to the dentist very soon to save the tooth.)

◆ Provide care until the ambulance personnel or the parents or guardians arrive and take over.

◆ Fill out the Babysitter's Report Record (pp. 22–23).

◆ Report to the parents or guardians when they arrive.

Muscle, Bone, and Joint Injuries

Notes

- Often, only medical personnel can tell what type and degree of injury occurred.

- You do not need to know what kind of injury it is to give first aid.

First Aid Steps

CHECK the scene and the infant or child. Use disposable gloves when you might touch any body fluid.

CALL 9-1-1 for the following situations:

- The involved limb is bent in the wrong shape.

- It feels or sounds like bones are rubbing together.

- You or the child heard a snap or pop when the injury happened.

- The infant or child cannot move or use the part normally.

- The injured area feels cold and numb.

- The injury involves the head, neck, or back.

- The cause of the injury makes it seem severe.

- There is a lot of swelling or a big bruise.

- You can see bone in the wound.
- The injured infant or child has trouble breathing.

CARE for the infant or child:
- Do not move the injured part.
- Apply a cold pack, such as ice in a plastic bag. Place a cloth or towel between the skin and the cold pack.
- Control any bleeding (see Bleeding, p. 113).

◆ Call the parents or guardians, explain the infant's or child's condition, and ask them to return home immediately.

◆ Provide care until the ambulance personnel or the parents or guardians arrive and take over.

◆ Fill out the Babysitter's Report Record (pp. 22–23).

◆ Report to the parents or guardians when they arrive.

See also Bleeding, p. 113.

Nosebleed

Notes
- A nosebleed is often caused by a blow to the nose.
- It also may be caused by an allergy, cold, nose picking, or dry mucous membranes.
- Bleeding may be heavy at first.

First Aid Steps

CHECK the scene and the infant or child. Use disposable gloves when you might touch any body fluid.

CALL 9-1-1 if bleeding cannot be controlled or if you suspect a head, neck, or back injury (see Head, Neck, and Back Injuries, pp. 128–129).

CARE for the infant or child:
- Have the child lean slightly forward.
- You or the child should pinch the nostrils together for about 10 minutes.
- Apply a cold pack, such as ice in a plastic bag, to the bridge of the nose. Place a cloth or towel between the skin and the cold pack.

- If the bleeding does not stop, put pressure on the upper lip just under the nose.
- When the bleeding stops, discourage the child from rubbing, blowing, or picking his or her nose.

◆ If bleeding does not stop, call the parents or guardians, explain the infant's or child's condition, and ask them to return home immediately.

◆ Provide care until the ambulance personnel or the parents or guardians arrive and take over.

◆ Fill out the Babysitter's Report Record (pp. 22–23).

◆ Report to the parents or guardians when they arrive.

Poisoning

Notes
- Any substance is a poison if it causes injury or illness if it enters the body.
- A poison can get into the body by being swallowed, breathed in, touched, or injected.
- The Poison Control Center can give information about most poisonous substances and tell you what to do.

First Aid Steps

CHECK the scene and the infant or child. Use disposable gloves when you might touch any body fluid or the poison.

CALL 9-1-1. Have someone else call if possible.

CARE for the infant or child:
- Move the infant or child to safety, away from the source of the poison.
- Care for any life-threatening conditions first (see Unconscious, Checking an Infant or Child, pp. 138–140; Rescue Breathing, Child, pp. 134–135; Rescue Breathing, Infant, pp. 135–136).
- Do not give the infant or child anything to eat or drink unless told to do so by the Poison Control Center or 9-1-1 dispatcher.
- If the infant or child vomits, put the infant or child on his or her side (see Vomiting, p. 140).

◆ Call the parents or guardians, explain the infant's or child's condition, and ask them to come home immediately.

- Provide care until the ambulance personnel or the parents or guardians arrive and take over.
- Fill out the Babysitter's Report Record (pp. 22–23).
- Report to the parents or guardians when they arrive.

Rescue Breathing, Child

Notes
- If a child stops breathing, you must breathe for him or her.
- When breathing stops, you cannot see, feel, or hear breaths; the chest does not rise and fall; and the skin becomes pale, ashen, or bluish.

First Aid Steps

CHECK the scene and the child. Use disposable gloves when you might touch any body fluid.

CALL 9-1-1 after 1 minute of care if you are alone. Have someone else call if possible.

CARE for the child:

- Tap the child on the shoulder and shout to see if he or she responds.
- If there is no response, tilt the head back slightly while lifting the chin.
- Look, listen, and feel for breathing for about 5 seconds.

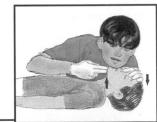

- If the child is not breathing, pinch the nose shut, and give 2 slow breaths.
- Check for a pulse at the side of the neck for about 5 to 10 seconds.

- If the child is not breathing but has a pulse, give 1 slow breath every 3 seconds.
- Give breaths for 1 minute (about 20 breaths).

- Call 9-1-1 if you have not already called.

- Recheck the pulse and breathing about every minute.
- Keep doing rescue breathing until the child starts breathing or the ambulance personnel arrive and take over.

◆ Call the parents or guardians as soon as the ambulance personnel arrive and take over.

◆ Provide care until the ambulance personnel or the parents or guardians arrive and take over.

◆ Fill out the Babysitter's Report Record (pp. 22–23).

◆ Report to the parents or guardians when they arrive.

Rescue Breathing. Infant

Notes
- If an infant stops breathing, you must breathe for the him or her.
- When breathing stops, you cannot see, feel, or hear breaths; the chest does not rise and fall; and the skin becomes pale, ashen, or bluish.

First Aid Steps

CHECK scene and the infant. Use disposable gloves when you might touch any body fluid.

CALL 9-1-1 after 1 minute of care if you are alone. Have someone else call if possible.

CARE for the infant:

- Tap the infant on the shoulder and shout to see if he or she responds.
- If there is no response, tilt the head back slightly while lifting the chin.
- Look, listen, and feel for breathing for about 5 seconds.
- If the infant is not breathing, cover the infant's nose and mouth with your mouth, and give 2 slow breaths.
- Check for a pulse on the inside of the upper arm for about 5 to 10 seconds.

- If the infant is not breathing but has a pulse, give 1 slow breath every 3 seconds.
- Give breaths for 1 minute (about 20 breaths).

◆ Call 9-1-1 if you have not already called.

- Recheck the pulse and breathing about every minute.
- Keep doing rescue breathing until the infant starts breathing or the ambulance personnel arrive and take over.

◆ Call the parents or guardians as soon as the ambulance personnel arrive and take over.

◆ Provide care until the ambulance personnel or the parents or guardians arrive and take over.

◆ Fill out the Babysitter's Report Record (pp 22–23).

◆ Report to the parents or guardians when they arrive.

Seizures

Notes
- Some infants or children have **seizure** problems that their parents or guardians are aware of.
- Follow any specific instructions from parents or guardians on what to do if the infant or child has a seizure.

First Aid Steps

CHECK the scene and the infant or child. Use disposable gloves when you might touch any body fluid.

CALL 9-1-1. Have someone else call if possible.

CARE for the infant or child:

- Remove any safety-related problems from around the infant or child during the seizure.
- Protect the infant's or child's head during the seizure by putting a thin cushion, such as a folded towel, under it.
- Roll the infant or child onto his or her side to allow fluids, such as saliva, blood, or vomit, to drain from the mouth.

- **NEVER** put anything in the infant's or child's mouth.
- After the seizure, help the infant or child rest comfortably in a quiet place. The infant or child may be sleepy afterward.
- Help clean the infant or child if a toileting accident occurred during the seizure.
- Check to see if the infant or child was injured during the seizure.

◆ Call the parents or guardians as soon as the ambulance personnel arrive and take over.

◆ Provide care until the ambulance personnel or the parents or guardians arrive and take over.

◆ Fill out the Babysitter's Report Record (pp. 22–23).

◆ Report to the parents or guardians when they arrive.

Splinter

First Aid Steps

CHECK the scene and the infant or child. Use disposable gloves when you might touch any body fluid.

CARE for the infant or child:

- Wash the area with soap and water.
- Have the child sit where you have good light and the child can rest the affected body part on a firm surface.
- Using tweezers, grasp the splinter as close to the skin as possible, and pull it out in the same direction it went in.
- Wash the wound again with soap and water.
- Cover the wound with an adhesive strip bandage.

If you cannot remove the splinter—

- Wash the wound, and cover it.
- Do not try to dig or cut the splinter out.
- Wait for the parents or guardians to remove the splinter when they return home.

◆ Provide care until the parents or guardians arrive and take over.

◆ Fill out the Babysitter's Report Record (pp. 22–23).

◆ Report to the parents or guardians when they arrive.

Stomachache

Notes

- A stomachache can be caused by many things, including spoiled food, overeating, constipation, or stress.

First Aid Steps

CHECK the scene and the infant or child. Use disposable gloves when you might touch any body fluid.

CALL 9-1-1 if the pain is severe.

CARE for the infant or child:

- Help the infant or child rest comfortably and put a container nearby if the child needs to vomit.

◆ Call the parents or guardians if the infant or child has a fever, difficulty urinating, or a long-lasting stomachache. Explain the infant's or child's condition, and ask the parents or guardians to return home.

◆ Provide care until the ambulance personnel or the parents or guardians arrive and take over.

◆ Fill out the Babysitter's Report Record (pp. 22–23).

◆ Report to the parents or guardians when they arrive.

See also Vomiting, p. 140.

Unconscious, Checking an Infant or Child

First Aid Steps

CHECK the scene and the infant or child. Use disposable gloves when you might touch any body fluid.

CALL 9-1-1 after 1 minute of care if you are alone. Have someone else call if possible.

CARE for the infant or child:

- Tap the infant or child on the shoulder and shout to see if he or she responds.

- If there is no response, tilt the head back slightly while lifting the chin.

- Look, listen, and feel for breathing for about 5 seconds.

If the infant or child is not breathing—

- Give 2 slow breaths.

    For a child, pinch the nose shut and make a seal over the child's mouth with your mouth.

    For an infant, make a seal over the infant's nose and mouth with your mouth.

- Check for a pulse for 5 to 10 seconds, and look for severe bleeding.

    For a child, check for a pulse at the side of the neck.

    For an infant, check for a pulse on the inside of the upper arm.

- Check for severe bleeding.

    Look over the infant or child from head to toe for signs of bleeding.

- If there is no pulse, begin CPR (see CPR, Child, pp. 123–125; CPR, Infant, pp. 125–126).

- If there is a pulse but the infant or child is not breathing, breathe for the infant or child—1 breath every 3 seconds (see Rescue Breathing, Child, pp. 134–135; Rescue Breathing, Infant, pp. 135–136).

- If the infant or child vomits or has a seizure, roll him or her onto the side to keep the airway open and allow fluids to drain from the mouth.

◆ Call the parents or guardians as soon as the ambulance personnel arrive and take over.

◆ Provide care until the ambulance personnel or the parents or guardians arrive and take over.

◆ Fill out the Babysitter's Report Record (pp. 22–23).

◆ Report to the parents or guardians when they arrive.

See also Rescue Breathing, Child, pp. 134–135; Rescue Breathing, Infant, pp. 135–136; CPR, Child, pp. 123–125; CPR, Infant, pp. 125–126.

Vomiting

First Aid Steps

CHECK the scene and the infant or child. Use disposable gloves when you might touch any body fluid.

CALL 9-1-1 if the infant or child vomits blood or is unconscious.

CARE for the infant or child:

- Put a bowl or basin nearby in case the child needs to vomit more.

- Clean the infant or child. Help the child rinse his or her mouth and blow his or her nose as needed.

- Let the child sip water every 5 minutes for 30 to 60 minutes. For an infant, offer a bottle with room temperature water.

- Help the infant or child rest comfortably.

- If the infant or child is unconscious, roll him or her onto the side (the recovery position) to allow the vomit to drain from the mouth.

◆ **Call** parents or guardians if the infant or child vomits more than once. Explain the infant's or child's condition. Ask the parents or guardians to come home.

◆ Provide care until the ambulance personnel or the parents or guardians arrive and take over.

◆ Fill out the Babysitter's Report Record (pp. 22–23).

◆ Report to the parents or guardians when they arrive.

See also Stomachache, p. 138.

Wounds, with Object

Notes

- A wound with an object stuck in it will be more difficult to care for than other wounds.
- Do not remove an object, such as a nail, large piece of glass, or knife, since it could cause more bleeding and further harm.

First Aid Steps

CHECK the scene and the infant or child. Use disposable gloves when you might touch any body fluid.

CALL 9-1-1. Have someone else call if possible.

CARE for the infant or child:

- Do not remove the object (except for dirt or a splinter; see Splinter, p. 137).
- Bandage bulky dressings (rolls of gauze) around the object to hold it in place.
- Bandage the dressing in place.
- Control the bleeding (see Bleeding, pp. 113–114).

◆ Call the parents or guardians, explain the infant's or child's condition, and ask them to come home immediately.

◆ Provide care until the ambulance personnel or the parents or guardians arrive and take over.

◆ Fill out the Babysitter's Report Record (pp. 22–23).

◆ Report to the parents or guardians when they arrive.

GLOSSARY

Accident: Any unexpected or unplanned event that may result in injury, death or a combination of serious effects.

Airway: The pathway through which air moves from the mouth and nose to the lungs.

Allergic reaction: A negative reaction of the body to certain insect stings, foods, or medications.

Ashen: Absence of color or grayish color; darker skin often looks ashen instead of pale.

Asthma: A condition that narrows the air passages and makes breathing difficult.

Bite: An injury to the skin caused by an insect, animal, or human.

Body fluids: Liquid substances produced by the body, including urine, saliva, and blood.

Check-Call-Care: Three action steps you take in an emergency.

Chemical hot pack: A sealed pouch with chemicals inside. The hot pack warms up when the chemicals are mixed together or the pouch is taken out of its plastic package.

Child abuse: The physical, psychological, or sexual assault on a child, resulting in injury or emotional trauma.

Choking: An emergency in which an infant or child cannot cough, speak, cry, or breathe because the airway is partly or completely blocked.

Cold pack: A waterproof package containing ice or other frozen solids used in first aid to prevent or treat swelling.

Conscious: When a person is awake and is not asleep or has not fainted. The person will breathe and be aware of his or her surroundings.

Constipation: The inability to have a bowel movement.

Crowing: A form of hoarse crying.

Cut: A break in the skin's surface.

Developmental stages: The stages a person goes through from birth to old age; each stage involves physical, mental, emotional, and social changes.

Discipline: Actions taken to guide a child to better behavior.

Disposable gloves: Thin, waterproof gloves worn to keep germs from the hands when contacting any body fluid, such as blood or vomit.

Diversity: The differences found among people.

Drowning: Death by suffocation when submerged in water.

Emergency: A problem situation where action is needed right away because someone is injured or ill.

Environments: Surroundings or conditions.

Face mask-face shield: A protective breathing device used during rescue breathing that prevents contact with blood or other body fluids.

Feces: Solid body waste from the digestive tract.

First aid: Care given to someone who is hurt or sick until more advanced care can be obtained. When provided in the first few minutes of an emergency, it can save a life.

First Aid Action Plan: A plan that explains how to take care of different kinds of injuries and illnesses.

Flammable: Something that can easily catch on fire.

Formula: A milk-based or soybean-based liquid mixture given to infants using a baby bottle.

Germs: A tiny living organism that cannot be seen by the human eye. Some germs may cause infection and disease, others may be harmless, and some may even be useful.

Heartbeat: The beat felt in arteries with each contraction of the heart. Also called pulse.

Hygiene: Activities like brushing your teeth or washing your hair that everyone needs to do to stay clean and healthy.

Infant: A baby younger than 12 months old.

Infectious: Able to cause disease.

Leader: Someone who acts responsibly and takes charge of a situation.

Minor bleeding: Bleeding that usually stops by itself within a few minutes.

Pale: Absence of color.

Poison Control Center: A special health care center that gives information to the public in cases of poisoning or suspected poisoning emergencies.

Poisoning: Eating, drinking, breathing, or injecting a substance that is solid, liquid, or gas that can severely injure or even kill you when taken into the body or put on the surface of the skin.

Preschooler: A child 3 to 5 years old.

Pulse: The beat felt in arteries with each contraction of the heart. Also called **heartbeat.**

Puncture wound: An injury to the skin caused by piercing with a pointed object.

Recovery position: Lying on one side with the face angled toward the ground to protect the airway in case of vomiting.

Rescue breathing: A method of breathing for someone who cannot.

Resume: A list of one's experience, skills, and abilities for doing a job.

Role model: Someone who acts in a responsible way for others to imitate.

Rubber pants: Waterproof garment worn over an infant's diaper to prevent leakage of body wastes.

Safety covers: Plastic protective covers put into or over an electrical outlet to prevent children from being shocked or burned.

Safety gate: A low, often removable gate to keep infants and toddlers away from stairs or other dangerous areas.

Safety rails or sides: The bars or slats on the side of a crib or bed that prevent an infant or child from falling out.

School-aged child: A child 5 to 8 years old.

Scrape: A wound where the skin has been rubbed away.

Security bars: Window or door bars that protect a home from intruders and are locked from the inside.

Seizure: The sudden attack of a disease or a condition usually resulting from disturbed electrical output in the brain.

Severe bleeding: Bleeding that squirts from the wound or cannot be easily controlled.

Sterile: Free from germs.

Strangulation: Blocking the airway by constricting it; cutting off someone's breathing.

Suffocation: Not being able to breathe.

Toddler: A child 1 to 3 years old.

Toileting: The process of urinating or having a bowel movement. A child usually is toilet trained between 2 to 5 years of age.

Unconscious: A person who is not awake or has fainted. The person is not aware of his or her surroundings and may or may not be breathing.

Urine: Liquid body waste.

Vomit: To throw up what is in the stomach through the mouth.

Wheezing: A hoarse, whistling sound during breathing that usually signals a breathing problem.

Wound: An injury to the soft tissues.

INDEX

MISSION OF THE AMERICAN RED CROSS

The American Red Cross, a humanitarian organization led by volunteers and guided by its Congressional Charter and the Fundamental Principles of the International Red Cross Movement, will provide relief to victims of disaster and help people prevent, prepare for, and respond to emergencies.

ABOUT THE AMERICAN RED CROSS

To support the mission of the American Red Cross, over 1.3 million paid and volunteer staff serve in some 1,600 chapters and blood centers throughout the United States and its territories and on military installations around the world. Supported by the resources of a national organization, they form the largest volunteer service and educational force in the nation. They serve families and communities through blood services, disaster relief and preparedness education, services to military family members in crisis, and health and safety education.

The American Red Cross provides consistent, reliable education and training in injury and illness prevention and emergency care, providing training to nearly 16 million people each year in first aid, CPR, swimming, water safety, and HIV/AIDS education.

All of these essential services are made possible by the voluntary services, blood and tissue donations, and financial support of the American people.

FUNDAMENTAL PRINCIPLES OF THE INTERNATIONAL RED CROSS AND RED CRESCENT MOVEMENT

HUMANITY

IMPARTIALITY

NEUTRALITY

INDEPENDENCE

VOLUNTARY SERVICE

UNITY

UNIVERSALITY